Word
Beyond the Basics

P.M. Heathcote

Published by
PG Online Limited
The Old Coach House
35 Main Road
Tolpuddle
Dorset
DT2 7EW
United Kingdom

sales@pgonline.co.uk
www.pgonline.co.uk

2018

PG ONLINE

Acknowledgements

FLYING MACHINE: CONSTRUCTION AND OPERATION
By W.J. Jackman and Thos. H. Russell 1912

Cover picture © 'Seasalt and Sand Study 2' 2016
Mixed media on linen 10cm x 10cm
Reproduced with the kind permission of Poppy Cyster.

https://poppycyster.com

Graphics and typesetting by PG Online Ltd.
First edition 2018

A catalogue entry for this book is available from the British Library

ISBN: 978-1-910523-12-4

Printed on FSC certified paper.
Printed by Bell and Bain Ltd, Glasgow, UK.

Preface

Microsoft Word is one of the most useful applications for anyone who uses a computer in their studies, at work or at home. However, a great many people have never been taught the best or most efficient way of performing simple tasks such as creating a neat list in columns, placing images exactly where they want them or quickly changing text styles throughout a document. Additionally, many users struggle to adapt to newer versions of Word, and need help learning the best ways of doing familiar tasks or using new facilities introduced in Word 2013 and subsequent versions.

This book assumes that you know the basics of how to create and edit a simple document, and shows you how to do much, much more. The mysteries of the tabs and ribbon interface used in Word 2013 and Word 2016 are laid bare. You will soon find you can do all you wanted and more in a fraction of the time it took before. It really is all very simple once it's explained!

Find out why you never again need to press the space bar two or more consecutive times when creating tabular lists, how to type accents or fractions, how to create reports with different headers and footers in different sections of the document, how to group and manipulate graphics, draw lines that are precisely horizontal or vertical, and use keyboard shortcuts to speed up common tasks.

How to use this book

You can work through the book from start to finish, pick out a particular chapter or simply use the book as a quick reference guide. A comprehensive index will help you find the information you are looking for.

You can learn and practise the skills using your own documents or use the documents provided in the folder **WBTB exercise documents** which you can download from the website **www.pgonline.co.uk** and save on your own computer.

Contents

Chapter 4 – Tabs and lists 27

Chapter 5 – Inserting images 35

Chapter 6 – Inserting shapes 43

Chapter 7 – Tables 53

Objectives

▶ Open a new blank document

▶ Get familiar with the various parts of the window

▶ Recognise the quick access toolbar, ribbon tabs, ribbon, ruler, scroll bar, status bar

▶ Choose a page layout for a new document

▶ Save and close a document

Starting Word

This book refers to **Word 2016**, part of **Office 365**. However, you will find very few differences between this version and Word 2010 or Word 2013 that will affect your use of this book.

You can load Microsoft Word in different ways:

● Click the **Word** icon in the Taskbar at the bottom of the screen, if it is there.

● Double-click the icon on the desktop, if it is there.

● Click the **Windows** icon at the bottom left of the screen. Click **Microsoft Office 2016.** and then choose **Word 2016**.

● Type **Word** into the search box in the Taskbar and select **Word 2016**.

When you open Word, you can either open a blank document, use a template, open a recent file or open another file stored online or on your computer.

From time to time as you use this book, you will be asked to open a file which you can download from the website **www.pgonline.co.uk**. You should download the folder containing all these files and save it somewhere on your computer for future use.

The screenshot on the next page shows the opening screen that appears when you launch Word and choose **Blank Document**.

The opening screen

The opening screen will be displayed. The appearance of the ribbon partly depends on the width of your document, so it may not be identical to the screen shown in **Figure 1.1**. If the ruler is not shown, select **View**, **Ruler**.

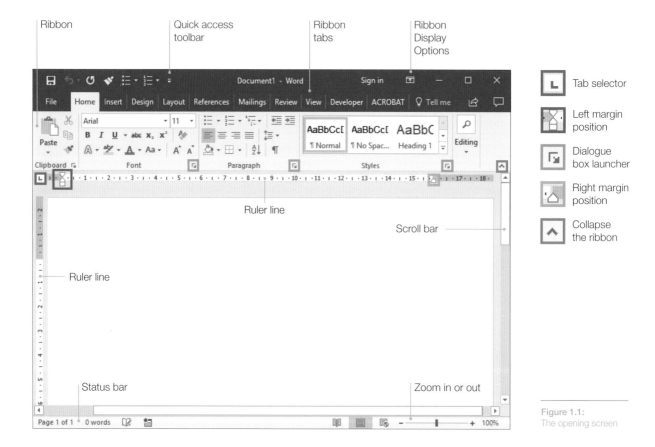

Figure 1.1:
The opening screen

▶ The **ribbon**, located underneath the **ribbon tabs**, contains the tools for each of the ribbon tabs, **File**, **Home**, **Insert**, **Design** and so on. The ribbon will change its appearance depending on which ribbon tab is selected. In the screenshot, the **Home** tab is selected.

▶ Tools on the ribbon are displayed in groups, for example the **Clipboard** group, **Font** group, **Paragraph** group and **Styles** group. Further options in each group are displayed by clicking the **dialogue box launcher**, the small arrow at the bottom right of each group.

▶ The ribbon can be hidden, or "collapsed", if you need more space, and restored using one of the **Ribbon Display Options**.

Setting page layout options

When you open a new document, it will be the default page size, **Portrait** rather than **Landscape** orientation, and have default margins. Any of these may be changed by clicking the **Layout** tab and selecting appropriate options from the ribbon.

Figure 1.2:
Page Layout ribbon

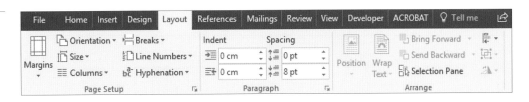

● Clicking **Orientation** will display an option box:

Figure 1.3:
Selecting an
orientation

▶ Clicking **Size** will present you with a series of pre-set options including A4, A5 and several more standard sizes, as well as an option **More Paper Sizes** where you can set your own custom size.

☐	**Letter** 21.59 cm x 27.94 cm
☐	**Legal** 21.59 cm x 35.56 cm
☐	**Executive** 18.41 cm x 26.67 cm
☐	**A3** 29.7 cm x 42 cm
☐	**A4** 21 cm x 29.7 cm
☐	**A5** 14.8 cm x 21 cm

Figure 1.4:
Choosing a paper size

Setting margins

Clicking **Margins** will display a range of pre-set margin sizes and an option **Custom margins**… allowing you to set your own margin sizes. The default margins are suitable for many documents but sometimes you may want to have narrower margins, or less space at the top or bottom of a document.

Figure 1.5:
Setting margin options

Mirrored margins

Select Mirror margins if your document will be printed double-sided and bound in the form of a report, pamphlet or book. This enables you to have page numbers always on the outside edge of a page (on the left-hand side for even-numbered pages, on the right for odd-numbered pages). You can also set different headers and footers on odd and even pages. See Chapter 9 for setting headers and footers.

Saving a document

Once you have created a new document with the desired settings, you should name and save it. You should save frequently to avoid losing too much work in the event of the computer crashing for any reason.

▶ Click the **File** tab, and a new screen appears.

▶ If this is the first time you are saving a document, you can click either **Save** or **Save As**. If it has already been saved, clicking **Save** will overwrite the previous saved version, and **Save As** will enable you to save a new version with a different name.

The shortcut key for saving is **Ctrl-S**.

Figure 1.6:
File options

Once you click **Save As**, you will see a **Browse** button and a list of recent folders. You can then select a folder and give the document a name.

Closing a document

You can close a document, and close Word at the same time, by pressing the **Close** icon ✕ in the top right corner of the document window.

If you have one only document open, you can close it without closing Word by selecting **Close** from the **File** options. This saves time by not having to reload Word if you are going to be working on another document before ending your session.

When you reopen a document, you will be able to pick up where you left off by clicking on the icon in the right margin:

Welcome back!
Pick up where you left off:

Selecting an online image
Yesterday

Printing a document

It's always wise to save before you print. It can sometimes happen that the print setup or process can cause your computer to crash, and if it is not saved you will lose it.

To print, click the **File** tab and select **Print**. You will be able to choose whether to print the entire document or just particular pages.

- To print pages 1-6 of a 10-page document, specify **1-6** in the **Pages** box.

- To print pages 1, 3 and 5-10, specify **1,3,5-10** in the **Pages** box.

Figure 1.7:
Printing a document

Print preview

On the right-hand side of the screen is a preview of how the document will look when printed. You can scroll through the pages to see what is on each page, and zoom in and out using the scroll bar.

Objectives

► Select, edit, copy and paste text

► Navigate around a document

► Spell-check a document

Opening an existing document

For the purposes of this chapter you will find it useful to have open a document which has more than one page, if you want to try out the Word features described. Click the **File** tab, select **Open** and open the document **Ch 2 Constructing a gliding machine.docx**, which is in the folder **WBTB exercise documents** downloadable from the website **www.pgonline.co.uk**.

Selecting text

The most common method of selecting text is to hold down the left mouse button while you drag the cursor across the text to be selected. Text and objects may be selected using the **Select** menu on the **Home** tab. Display the **Home** tab and click **Select** from the **Editing** group at the right-hand end of the ribbon.

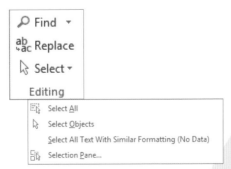

Figure 2.1:
Selecting text
or objects

The **Select** menu is useful when you want to select an entire document. However, a quicker way to do this is to use the shortcut key combination **Ctrl-A**.

Table 1 below shows several alternative ways of selecting text.

- Practise each of the selection methods on your open document.

Table 1

Operation	Method
Select a word	Double-click anywhere in the word
Select one or more lines	Click in the left margin to select a line. Drag down the margin to select several lines
Select a sentence	Hold down **Ctrl** and click anywhere in the sentence
Select a paragraph	Triple-click anywhere in the paragraph
Select an entire document	From the **Select** menu in the **Editing** group at the right-hand end of the ribbon, choose **Select All**. Or, use the shortcut key combination **Ctrl-A**
Select a large block of text	Click at the beginning of the text, scroll down to the end of the text you want to select, then hold down **Shift** while you click
Select all text from current location to the end of the document	Click at the start point, then click **Ctrl-Shift-End**
Select non-adjacent text	Select the first piece of text, then hold down **Ctrl** while you select another piece of text
Select a rectangular area of text	Hold down **Alt** while you drag across the text

The last tip on how to select a rectangular area of text is useful if, for example, you have a tabbed list and want to embolden one column, as in the following example.

	Wood	**Weight per cubic ft. in lbs.**	**Tensile Strength lbs. per sq. in.**	**Compressive Strength lbs. per sq in.**
Select first column →	Hickory	53	12,000	8,500
	Oak	50	12,000	9,000
	Ash	38	12,000	6,000
	Walnut	38	8,000	6,000
	Spruce	25	8,000	5,000
	Pine	25	5,000	4,500

Figure 2.2:
Selecting a column

Copying, moving and pasting text

- To copy text, first select it and then press **Ctrl-C** or click the **Copy** icon next to the **Paste** icon on the **Home** tab ribbon.

- To paste the text, click where it is to be copied and press **Ctrl-V** or click the **Paste** icon.

- To move text rather than copying it, press **Ctrl-X** rather than **Ctrl-C** and then paste the text.

Using drag and drop

A quick way of moving text from one location to another is to select it and then click and hold while you drag it to its new location.

To copy the selection rather than moving it, hold down **Ctrl** while you drag.

Using the clipboard

If you are planning to copy some text to several places in your document, you can open the clipboard so that you can see all the items you have copied. Whenever you copy something, it will appear in the clipboard. To paste any item in the clipboard to the current cursor location, click the item in the clipboard.

- Click the down-arrow at the bottom right-hand corner of the **Clipboard** group to display the clipboard.

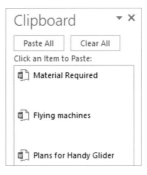

Figure 2.3:
The clipboard

Finding text

To find a word or phrase in your text, click **Find** in the **Editing** group and type in the word you want to find. The shortcut for this is **Ctrl-F**.

The Navigation pane will open with the **Results** tab selected, allowing you to type in the word you want to find. All the results will then be displayed, and you can select any of them.

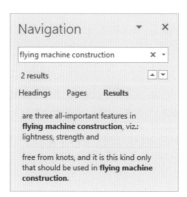

Figure 2.4:
The Navigation pane

Finding and replacing text

To replace text such as a name, for example, through a document, select the text and click the **Replace** button at the right-hand end of the ribbon. If it is not visible, click the down-arrow under the **Editing** icon to see it.

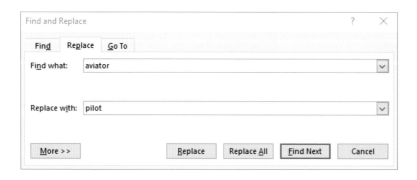

Figure 2.5:
Find and Replace

Replacing special characters such as line breaks

If you have copied text from a .pdf document, it will have line breaks at the end of every line, so that every line is effectively a new paragraph. This can be very annoying if it is a long document that you want to format for a different page or margin width.

You can display non-printing characters such as **Enter** (i.e. a line break or new paragraph marker) by clicking the pilcrow ¶ (**Show/Hide**) icon in the paragraph group. Hide non-printing characters by pressing it again.

To replace all the line breaks in a document with single spaces, so that the text appears in a single paragraph:

- Click **Replace** in the **Editing** group.
- With the cursor in the **Find what** field, click **More>>** and then **Special**, select **Paragraph mark** from the top of the list.
- In the **Replace with** field, press the space bar once.
- Click **Replace All**.
- Click **OK**.

Undoing an edit

If you change your mind about an edit, you can undo it by pressing the **Undo** icon on the Quick Access toolbar at the top left of the window or by using the key combination **Ctrl-Z** . Repeated use of either of these will undo previous edits, so pressing **Ctrl-Z** three times, for example, will undo the previous three edits.

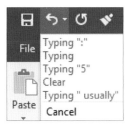

Figure 2.6:
Undoing edits

Selecting **Typing "usually"** in the above list of edits will undo this and all the edits above it in the list.

The edits can be redone by clicking the **Redo** button (clockwise arrow) in the Quick Access toolbar or **Ctrl-Y**.

Navigating around a document

- Using the scroll button on the mouse is the easiest way of moving a short distance backwards or forwards in your document.

- To move more than a page or so, it is more convenient to use the scroll bar on the right of the document. You can either drag the scroll bar, or click above or below it to move up or down a page at a time.

- Clicking the up- or down-arrow at the top or bottom of the scroll bar will move up or down one line at a time.

When you open an existing document in Word, pressing **Shift-F5** will take you directly to the place where you last entered or edited the document. When you are working on a document, pressing **Shift-F5** several times will cycle you through the last places where you made an edit.

Navigating a long document

If your document has many pages, you have several options for finding a specific place, using keys on the keyboard.

- **Page Up**   Move up one screen of text at a time
- **Page Down**   Move down one screen of text at a time
- **Ctrl-Home**   Go to the beginning of the document
- **Ctrl-End**   Go to the end of the document

Going to a specific page

You can go directly to a specific page using the shortcut **Ctrl-G** or by clicking **Editing, Replace** on the **Home** tab. Click the **Go To** tab to bring up the following dialogue box:

Figure 2.7:
Navigating to a
specified page

- Enter the number of the page that you wish to go to.

The View ribbon

The first group on the **View** ribbon is the **Views** group. Most of the time you will probably work in **Print Layout** view, which shows the document as it will appear when printed. Clicking **Read Mode** collapses the ribbon, giving more room on the screen to view your document. To return to **Print Layout** view and restore the ribbon, select **View**, **Edit document**.

The Show group

The **Show** group enables you to show or hide the ruler. Normally you will always have the ruler showing. If it is not visible, click the **Ruler** option in this group.

The **Navigation pane** provides another way of navigating around a long document. Using the **Headings** tab in this pane, it can display all the headings in a document, provided that you have used Heading styles (See Chapter 3).

Clicking the **Pages** tab displays a small image of each page. Click a page to go directly to it.

The **Results** tab will be displayed automatically when you select **Find** on the **Home** tab. Enter any word or phrase in the Search box and all occurrences will be listed. Selecting one will take you directly to it.

Zoom options

Using the **Zoom** options on the **View** ribbon, you can zoom in or out, and view multiple pages on the screen at once.

Note that you can also zoom in or out using the **Zoom** bar at the right-hand end of the **Status bar** at the bottom of the screen. Alternatively, hold down the **Ctrl** key while you scroll the mouse wheel.

Spell-checking a document

To try out the spell-checker, download the document **Ch 2 Spellcheck.docx** from the folder **WBTB exercise documents** downloadable from the website **www.pgonline.co.uk**. Or, type the following text, watching carefully as you type. Try misspelling the word "the" as "teh" and observe what happens.

You can spell-check the whole or part of a document.

- Position the cursor at the start of the text.

- Click the **Review** tab, and select **Spelling and Grammar** in the **Proofing** group at the left-hand end of the ribbon. Alternatively, press **F7**. Pressing **Shift-F7** will display a thesaurus.

Spell-checking

As you type, some words that you type wrongly are automatically corrected, possibly without you even noticing the changes. Other words which Word does not reconise may be underline with a red squiggle. Some words will not be picked out by the spell-checker even thiough they are wong in the context they are written.

Some common names like Bob, Anne, Henry, will be recognised as correct, and Hanry will be queried. Parris, Lundon, Florance may or may not be picked up by the spell-checker.

Figure 2.9:
Spell-checking a
document

The spell-checker will stop at each word that it does not recognise and offer suggestions, which you can accept by clicking one of the choices, **Ignore Once**, **Ignore All** or **Add to Dictionary**. Clicking the down-arrow next to a choice gives you further options.

Notice that the spell-checker does not pick up the wrongly spelt word **underline** in the third line, as it is a valid word although wrong in this context.

Correcting individual words

- To correct a word that has been underlined in red, right-click it and select from the options given by Word.

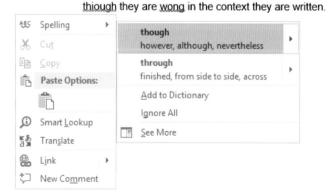

Figure 2.10:
Spelling options

Objectives

▶ Use and customise styles

▶ Select font style, size and characteristics

▶ Set line and paragraph spacing

▶ Use columns

▶ Insert column breaks and page breaks

▶ Show non-printing characters

Using styles

Clicking the **Home** tab displays the Formatting tools on the ribbon.

Figure 3.1:
Home ribbon

The five groups on this tab are:

● **Clipboard** for editing, copying and pasting text and formats

● **Font** for setting and amending type, size and characteristics of font

● **Paragraph** for setting and amending paragraph spacing, borders and more

● **Styles** for setting font styles

● **Editing** for finding, replacing and selecting text

Default styles

Using default Word styles has many advantages, particularly in a document of several pages in which you want to maintain a consistent appearance throughout and perhaps add a Table of Contents.

The screenshot in **Figure 3.2** shows a document that has used the default style called **Normal** throughout.

- Load the document, called **Ch 3 Top Cruise destinations.docx**, from the folder **WBTB exercise documents**, downloadable from the website **www.pgonline.co.uk**.

- Click the dialogue box launcher (down-arrow) at the bottom right of the **Styles** group in the ribbon to display the **Styles** pane at the right-hand side of the document.

- Click the **Show Preview** checkbox to see what the styles look like.

Figure 3.2:
Displaying styles

- To change the heading to **Title** style, click anywhere in the title **Three Top Cruise destinations** and click **Title** in the **Styles** pane to the right of the document.

- To change the style of the three paragraph headings **Caribbean**, **Antarctica** and **Mediterranean** to **Heading 1** style, hold down **Ctrl** while you double-click each of the headings to select them. Then click **Heading 1** in the style box.

Editing a style

You can change any of the given styles or create new styles of your own. The easiest way to do this is to format a word or paragraph as you would like it to appear throughout the document, and then right-click the style name in the **Styles** pane.

- Double-click the heading **Caribbean**, and select a new colour, for example **Dark Red**, for the heading.

- Click the **Increase Font Size** icon in the **Font** group and increase the font size to 18.

- Right-click **Heading 1** in the **Styles** pane. (You may need to click it twice.) A pop-up window appears.

- Select **Update Heading 1 to Match Selection**.

- All the headings will change automatically to the new style.

Figure 3.3:
Editing a style

Changing paragraph spacing

Select the first paragraph by triple-clicking within it, or dragging across the text. This is formatted in the default **Normal** style. Hover the cursor over **Normal** in the **Styles** pane to see the settings for the style.

The paragraph settings have been set to **1.08 lines**, (a little more than single spacing), and there is an **8pt** space after a paragraph in **Normal** style.

```
Normal:
Font
        FONT  (Default) Arial
Paragraph
        ALIGNMENT  Left
        SPACING
        Line spacing:  Multiple 1.08 li
        After:  8 pt
        LINE AND PAGE BREAKS  Widow/Orphan control
Style
        Style Show in the Styles gallery
```

Figure 3.4:
Normal style settings

Here's how to change the spacing to single spacing, with a 6-point space after the paragraph.

- With the first paragraph selected, click the down-arrow in the **Paragraph** group on the **Home** tab ribbon. Alternatively, right-click to display the pop-up window, and select **Paragraph**... Change settings as shown, and click **OK** to close the window.

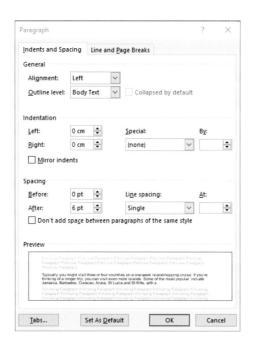

Figure 3.5:
Setting paragraph and line spacing

- Right-click **Normal** in the **Styles** pane and select **Update Normal to Match Selection**.

You can change the font or font size in a similar way.

Creating a new style

Suppose you want a new style which you will use to caption graphics that will be placed in the document. The new style will be **10pt Arial Italic, centred**.

- On a new line at the end of the document, type some text in the desired style, for example just the words *Picture caption*.

- To make the text italic, select it and click the *I* icon in the **Font** group, or **Ctlr-I**.

- To centre the text, select the text and click the **Centre** icon in the **Paragraph** group. **Ctlr-E** is the shortcut.

- Select this text and at the bottom of the **Styles** pane, click the **New Style** icon.

Figure 3.6:
Creating a new style

- A dialogue box will appear, allowing you to name the new style and make any changes.

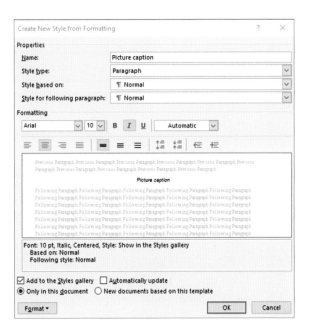

Figure 3.7:
Naming the new style

- Make any changes you want, name the style and click **OK**.

A new style named **Picture Caption** appears in the **Styles** pane.

Font styles

Using options in the **Font** group, you can make changes to the appearance of selected text.

A˄ A˅	Increase or decrease font size
Aa ▾	Change to uppercase, lowercase, sentence case and other options
A⬦	Remove all formatting from the selection, leaving it in default **Normal** style
B *I* <u>U</u>	Make text bold, italic or underlined in a choice of underline styles
a̶b̶c̶	Cross out text by drawing a line through it
x₂ x²	Subscript or Superscript text
Ⓐ ▾	Use text effects
ab⟋	Select a colour to highlight text
A ▾	Choose a text colour

Paragraph styles

Using options in the **Paragraph** group, you can create bulleted or numbered lists, indent or outdent text.

You can left justify, right justify, centre or justify selected text, and change line and paragraph spacing from the pop-up window which appears when you click the down-arrow next to the fifth icon on the second row (outlined in red in **Figure 3.8**).

You can also shade the area behind selected text and put a border around text.

Instead of using the icons, you can click the dialogue box launcher at the bottom left of the **Paragraph** group (outlined in blue in Figure 3.8) to display the window shown in **Figure 3.5**, and change settings in the window.

Figure 3.8:
Paragraph group

The easiest way to find out what every icon does is to try them out – use the document **Ch 3 Top Cruise destinations.docx**, or open one of your own, to try out all the options and then close without saving.

Using columns

When you start a new document, you can specify that it is to be formatted in two, three or more columns.

- On the **Layout** tab, hover over the **Columns** option in the **Page Setup** group to view the tooltip.

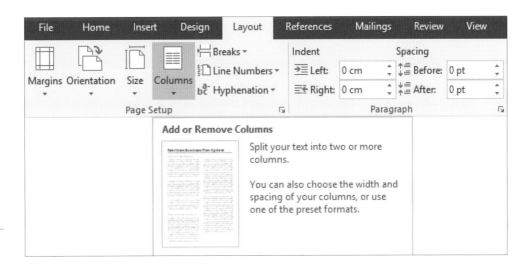

Figure 3.9:
The Columns option

Customising a column layout

Click the down-arrow underneath or next to **Columns** and select **More Columns**... A dialogue box appears in which you can format the columns as you want them, specifying the width of each column, the amount of space between the columns and whether or not you want a line between the columns.

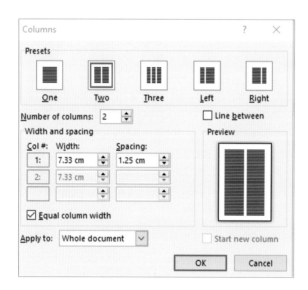

Figure 3.10:
Customising
column layout

Adding columns to an existing layout

You can type or import your text in a single column layout and then arrange some or all of it in columns.

- Open the document called **Ch 3 Top Cruise destinations with styles.docx** from the folder **WBTB exercise documents** downloadable from the website **www.pgonline.co.uk**, or use the document you have created. It should look something like **Figure 3.11**:

Three top cruise destinations

Caribbean

Typically you might visit three or four countries on a one-week island-hopping cruise. If you're thinking of a longer trip, you can visit even more islands. Some of the most popular include Jamaica, Barbados, Curaçao, Aruba, St Lucia and St Kitts, with stop-offs to lie on sandy beaches, participate in water sports or take tours to learn about the colourful history of each island.

For a different experience, Cuba is fascinating, and you'll need more than just a one-day stop-off – ships often sail round the island stopping for a day at different ports.

Antarctica

If you fancy a unique cruise to the coldest, most remote part of the earth, Antarctica with its vast, unspoiled landscapes and gigantic icebergs will take your breath away.

You'll cruise on a ship that holds no more than 200 passengers, and disembark to find yourself walking among penguins, getting close to sea lions and buckling on snowshoes for a walk across the spectacular landscape.

Mediterranean

Why not try a cruise to some of Europe's finest destinations, including Florence, Naples, Rome and Barcelona as well as some of the gems of the Mediterranean like St Tropez?

In Florence, you'll be able to gaze in wonder at Michelangelo's David. Walk around the famous city of Pompeii, buried under metres of lava from a volcanic eruption in 79 A.D., and climb to the crater rim of nearby Mount Vesuvius.

Figure 3.11:
Formatted document
with styles

- Select the first two paragraphs of text, click the **Columns** icon on the **Layout** ribbon and choose **Two columns**.

Figure 3.12:
Selecting number
of columns

Your document will now appear like this:

Three top cruise destinations

Caribbean

Typically you might visit three or four countries on a one-week island-hopping cruise. If you're thinking of a longer trip, you can visit even more islands. Some of the most popular include Jamaica, Barbados, Curaçao, Aruba, St Lucia and St Kitts, with stop-offs to lie on sandy beaches, participate in water sports or take tours to learn about the colourful history of each island.

For a different experience, Cuba is fascinating, and you'll need more than just a one-day stop-off – ships

often sail round the island stopping for a day at different ports.

Antarctica

If you fancy a unique cruise to the coldest, most remote part of the earth, Antarctica with its vast, unspoiled landscapes and gigantic icebergs will take your breath away.

You'll cruise on a ship that holds no more than 200 passengers, and disembark to find yourself walking among penguins, getting close to sea lions and buckling on snowshoes for a walk across the spectacular landscape.

Mediterranean

Why not try a cruise to some of Europe's finest destinations, including Florence, Naples, Rome and Barcelona as well as some of the gems of the Mediterranean like St Tropez?

In Florence, you'll be able to gaze in wonder at Michelangelo's David. Walk around the famous city of Pompeii, buried under metres of lava from a volcanic eruption in 79 A.D., and climb to the crater rim of nearby Mount Vesuvius.

Picture caption

Figure 3.13:
Two-column layout

Inserting a column break

The document could be improved by having the two headings **Caribbean** and **Antarctica** each at the top of a column. There needs to be a column break just before the heading **Antarctica**.

- Click just before the **A** of **Antarctica** to create a selection point. From the **Layout** ribbon tab select **Breaks, Column.**

You now need to line up the two headings by inserting some space above the heading **Antarctica**.

- Select the heading, right-click and choose **Paragraph…**
- Increase the **Spacing Before** to **18pt** and click **OK.**

Now the document appears like this:

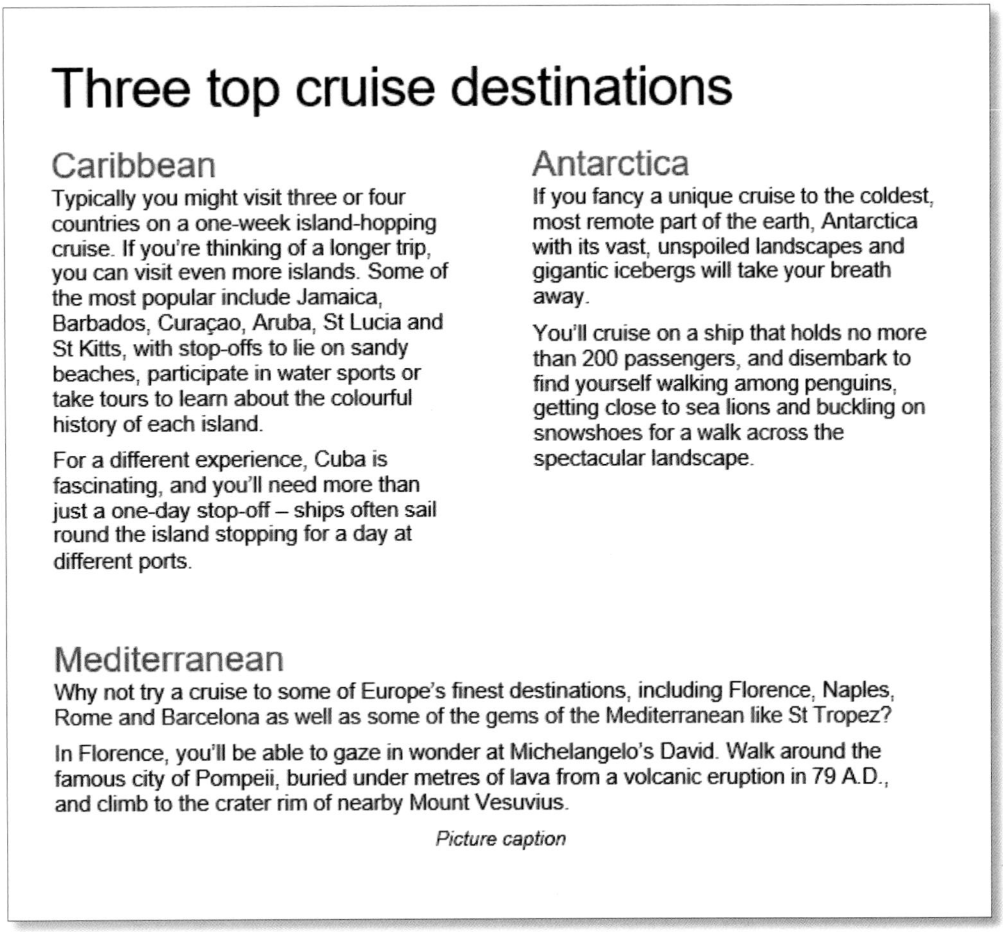

Three top cruise destinations

Caribbean

Typically you might visit three or four countries on a one-week island-hopping cruise. If you're thinking of a longer trip, you can visit even more islands. Some of the most popular include Jamaica, Barbados, Curaçao, Aruba, St Lucia and St Kitts, with stop-offs to lie on sandy beaches, participate in water sports or take tours to learn about the colourful history of each island.

For a different experience, Cuba is fascinating, and you'll need more than just a one-day stop-off – ships often sail round the island stopping for a day at different ports.

Antarctica

If you fancy a unique cruise to the coldest, most remote part of the earth, Antarctica with its vast, unspoiled landscapes and gigantic icebergs will take your breath away.

You'll cruise on a ship that holds no more than 200 passengers, and disembark to find yourself walking among penguins, getting close to sea lions and buckling on snowshoes for a walk across the spectacular landscape.

Mediterranean

Why not try a cruise to some of Europe's finest destinations, including Florence, Naples, Rome and Barcelona as well as some of the gems of the Mediterranean like St Tropez?

In Florence, you'll be able to gaze in wonder at Michelangelo's David. Walk around the famous city of Pompeii, buried under metres of lava from a volcanic eruption in 79 A.D., and climb to the crater rim of nearby Mount Vesuvius.

Picture caption

Figure 3.14:
Two-column layout with column break

Inserting a page break

You can insert a page break at any point in your document. For example, to start the heading **Mediterranean** on a new page, position the cursor at the start of the heading and use the shortcut key combination **Ctrl-Enter** to insert a page break. You can also do this by selecting **Breaks**, **Page** from the **Layout** ribbon tab.

Displaying and hiding non-printing characters

Sometimes it is hard to figure out why you have breaks where you don't want them.

- On the **Home** ribbon, click the **Paragraph mark** icon in the **Paragraph** group. You can then see the non-printing characters such as a space (signified by a dot), a new paragraph mark (¶) and column and page breaks.

- Delete any of these characters that you do not want using the **Delete** or **Backspace** keys.

- Hide the non-printing characters by pressing the **Paragraph mark** icon again.

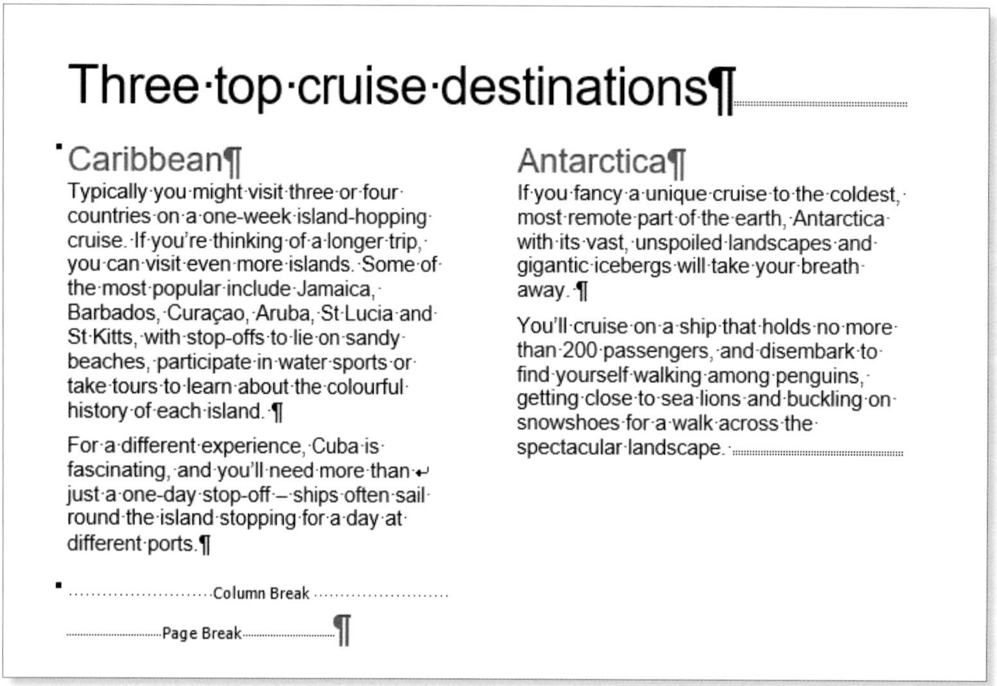

Three·top·cruise·destinations¶

·Caribbean¶

Typically·you·might·visit·three·or·four· countries·on·a·one-week·island-hopping· cruise.·If·you're·thinking·of·a·longer·trip,· you·can·visit·even·more·islands.·Some·of· the·most·popular·include·Jamaica,· Barbados,·Curaçao,·Aruba,·St·Lucia·and· St·Kitts,·with·stop-offs·to·lie·on·sandy· beaches,·participate·in·water·sports·or· take·tours·to·learn·about·the·colourful· history·of·each·island.·¶

For·a·different·experience,·Cuba·is· fascinating,·and·you'll·need·more·than·↵ just·a·one-day·stop-off·–·ships·often·sail· round·the·island·stopping·for·a·day·at· different·ports.¶

·····················Column Break······················

··············Page Break··············¶

Antarctica¶

If·you·fancy·a·unique·cruise·to·the·coldest,· most·remote·part·of·the·earth,·Antarctica· with·its·vast,·unspoiled·landscapes·and· gigantic·icebergs·will·take·your·breath· away.·¶

You'll·cruise·on·a·ship·that·holds·no·more· than·200·passengers,·and·disembark·to· find·yourself·walking·among·penguins,· getting·close·to·sea·lions·and·buckling·on· snowshoes·for·a·walk·across·the· spectacular·landscape.·

Figure 3.15:
Displaying non-printing characters

Objectives

▸ Set tabs and indents on the ruler line

▸ Create numbered and bulleted lists

Creating a list in columns

Creating a list of names, products, numbers etc., neatly laid out in columns is a very common operation. Here is a table taken from the document **Ch 4 Flying machines 1912 wind velocities** which is in the folder **WBTB Exercise documents** downloadable from **www.pgonline.co.uk.**

on an obstructed field difficult and uncertain. To handle a glider successfully the place of operation should be clear and the wind moderate and steady. If it is gusty postpone your flight. In this connection it will be well to understand the velocity of the wind, and what it means as shown in the following table:

Miles per hour	Feet per second	Pressure per sq. foot
10	14.7	.492
25	36.7	3.075
50	73.3	12.300
100	146.6	49.200

Pressure of wind increases in proportion to the square of the velocity. Thus wind at 10 miles

Figure 4.1:
Columns in a list

Displaying non-printing characters

You can display the non-printing characters to see how the list has been formatted by clicking the **Show/Hide** icon (¶) in the **Paragraph** group on the **Home** tab.

Displaying the non-printing characters in the list reveals that the columns of figures have been created with repeated use of the Space bar (denoted by a dot).

```
· · · · ·Miles ·per ·hour ·Feet ·per ·second · · · · ·Pressure ·per ·sq. ·foot¶
· · · · · · · · ·10 · · · · · · · · · · · · · · · · ·14.7 · · · · · · · · · · · · · · · · · .492¶
· · · · · · · · ·25 · · · · · · · · · · · · · · · · ·36.7 · · · · · · · · · · · · · · · ·3.075¶
· · · · · · · · ·50 · · · · · · · · · · · · · · · · ·73.3 · · · · · · · · · · · · · · ·12.300¶
· · · · · · · · ·100 · · · · · · · · · · · · · · ·146.6 · · · · · · · · · · · · · ·49.200¶
```

Figure 4.2:
Non-printing characters revealed

(To hide the non-printing characters, press the same symbol again.)

In the table, the columns are lined up neatly only because a non-proportional font, **Courier New**, has been used for the table, meaning that every character takes up exactly the same amount of space.

- Open the document and try changing the font in the table to **Times New Roman, 12pt**. The figures in the table are no longer exactly aligned.

Miles per hour	Feet per second	Pressure per sq. foot
10	14.7	.492
25	36.7	3.075
50	73.3	12.300
100	146.6	49.200

Figure 4.3:
Table in Times New Roman font

This is very unsatisfactory! If you ever find yourself typing more than one consecutive space, you should ask yourself whether you should be using a tab instead.

Incidentally, do NOT leave two spaces after a full stop. This is now considered outdated practice!

Setting tab stops

The easiest way to set tabs is to add tab stops on the ruler line.

Figure 4.4:
The tab selector and ruler line

At the left-hand end of the ruler is the **tab selector**, highlighted in red in **Figure 4.4**. Clicking repeatedly on the tab selector scrolls through the different types of tab stops available.

L	**Left tab**	– Text is aligned to the right of the tab stop.
⊥	**Centre tab**	– Text is centred on the tab as you type.
⅃	**Right tab**	– Text is right aligned at the tab.
⊥·	**Decimal tab**	– Numbers are aligned to the left of the decimal.
I	**Bar tab**	– This inserts a vertical bar at the tab position when the tab key is pressed. It is not used to position text.

When tabs are set, pressing the **Tab** key (above the **Caps Lock** key, to the left of the letter **Q** on the keyboard) moves the cursor to the next tab stop (**Shift** + **Tab** moves it back again). Tabs should always be used to keep text in a list correctly lined up. Using the space bar is not only inefficient and time-consuming, but also results in small variations in the positioning of text on different lines. Different characters take up different amounts of space (using proportional spacing) in all but a few fonts such as Courier.

To set a tab stop, click on the tab selector (and keep clicking on it until the desired tab stop shows) and then click in the ruler line at each point where you want a tab stop.

Note that if you do not set any tab stops, default tab spacing is set every half inch (1.27 cm). This spacing is overridden when you set your own tab stops.

- Copy and paste the table to a new document.

- Ignore the column headings for the moment, and select the four lines of numbers.

- Click the **Left tab** selector several times to scroll through the different types of tab. Stop when you get to the decimal tab. If you miss it, keep clicking until it comes round again.

- With the figures still selected, click in the ruler line at 2.5, 6.5 and 10.5, as shown in **Figure 4.5**, approximately above the decimal points in the list.

Replacing spaces with tabs

- Hold down the **Alt** key while you select all the spaces to the left of the first column. (Keep the non-printing characters displayed.)

- Press the **Delete** key to delete them all.

- Press the **Tab** key on the keyboard to insert a tab on each line before the first column.

- Repeat this procedure to replace the spaces between the other columns with tabs. You will need to delete a few extra spaces separately.

- Now deal with the headings line, setting appropriate **Centre** tabs to centre the text above the figures.

You should end up with a neat list, as shown below with the tabs for the heading line:

Figure 4.5:
Tabbed list

	Miles per hour	Feet per second	Pressure per sq. foot¶
→	10 →	14.7 →	.492¶
→	25 →	36.7 →	3.075¶
→	50 →	73.3 →	12.300¶
→	10 →	146.6 →	49.200¶

Changing the font in the list

If you now change the font of the list, including headings, to **Times New Roman, 12pt**, it appears as follows:

Miles per hour	Feet per second	Pressure per sq. foot
10	14.7	.492
25	36.7	3.075
50	73.3	12.300
10	146.6	49.200

Figure 4.6:
Tabbed list in Times
New Roman font

This time, the list converts perfectly to any other font.

Clearing tab stops

Tab stops can be removed by dragging them off the ruler line. They can be adjusted by dragging them along the ruler in either direction.

To clear all the tabs in one go, on the **Home** tab, in the **Paragraph** group click the arrow in the bottom right-hand corner to display the Paragraph dialogue box. Click the **Tabs…** button at the bottom of the window and click **Clear All**.

Using default tab stops

By default, left tab stops are set every half inch (1.27 cm). You can use these tab stops, but as soon as you set one of your own tab stops in a list that has been formatted using default stops, you may find that the list is all over the place. You need to delete all the extra previously placed tab stops.

Indents

At the left-hand end of the ruler line you will see the indent symbols:

1: The **first line indent** allows you to indent the first line of a paragraph.

2: The **hanging indent** allows you to indent the second and subsequent lines of a paragraph, which is very useful in creating many different kinds of list.

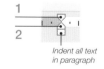

Indent all text
in paragraph

For example, look at the settings on the ruler line which could be used to create a list of tabs similar to the one on Page 28:

Decimal tab	Numbers are aligned to the left of the decimal.
Bar tab	This inserts a vertical bar at the tab position when the tab key is pressed. It is not used to position text.

Figure 4.7:
Setting a
hanging indent

A left tab has been set at 1.5 cm. The hanging indent symbol has been dragged to the 4cm position, so that the second line of each paragraph is automatically indented at this point.

To set a hanging indent, drag the hanging indent symbol (not the block underneath it) to the desired position.

To clear an indent, place the cursor at the start of the first line and press backspace.

Creating a bulleted list

A bulleted list can be quickly created by clicking the **Bullets** icon in the **Paragraph** group.

To change the appearance of the bullets, click the arrow to display the dialogue box:

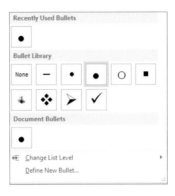

Figure 4.8:
Bullets

Here is a list created using the default bullet, showing the settings on the ruler line. Note the hanging indent:

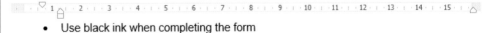

- Use black ink when completing the form
- Write your name and address in block capitals
- If there is not enough room to enter all the information on Page 3, continue on the blank sheet of paper provided
- Post the form in the envelope provided

Figure 4.9:
A simple
bullet-pointed list

The indents can be changed manually if, for example, you do not want the list to be indented.

Creating a numbered list

Numbered lists are useful in many different situations including, for example, instructions for what to do in a fire drill, how to assemble a piece of furniture, or a set of questions for a test or exam.

- Click the **Numbers** icon in the **Paragraph** group.

- As you type your list, each time you press **Enter** the new line will be assigned the next number.

Default indents and paragraph spacing are applied to the list as you type it. Try typing the following list:

> **Product designers may select materials on the basis of:**
>
> 1. cost
> 2. reliability
> 3. longevity
> 4. sustainability
> 5. recyclability

Figure 4.10:
A simple
numbered list

You can change the indents and paragraph spacing manually by selecting the list, right-clicking and selecting **Paragraph…** from the pop-up window.

One of the advantages of using automatic numbering is that you can change the order in which items appear and the numbering will automatically adjust.

- Double-click an item and drag it to a new position in the list. Note that the numbers remain in sequence.

- To change the format of the numbers, click the down-arrow on the **Numbering** icon to bring up a list of options as shown in **Figure 4.11**.

Figure 4.11:
Numbering options

You can insert an un-numbered sentence in the middle of the list and the numbers will again automatically adjust.

- To insert a sentence after item 3, press **Enter** at the end of item 3 to create a new line.

- Click the **Numbering** icon to deselect it.

- Enter the un-numbered line of text.

- Click the **Number** icon to restart the numbering, which will default to 1.

Product designers may select materials on the basis of:
1. cost
2. reliability
3. longevity

They may also consider:

1.

Continue Numbering

- Click the down-arrow which appears to the left of the number 1, and select **Continue Numbering**.

- Complete your list.

Product designers may select materials on the basis of:
1. cost
2. reliability
3. longevity

They may also consider:

4. sustainability
5. recyclability

An alternative and often quicker method is to type the list with all lines numbered, and then select the lines that are to be unnumbered and click the **Numbering** icon to deselect numbering on that line. All the other numbers in the list will automatically adjust.

The following example shows a more complex list in the form of a Maths test. Some of the questions have parts a, b… and some have paragraphs that are not numbered. Don't worry, you don't have to do the Maths test!

Maths test

1. Work out:

     a. $(5 + 3)^2$

     b. 4^3

2. A box of chocolates has 15 chocolates. There is one dark chocolate for every two white chocolates.

   How many chocolates in the box are

     a. dark

     b. white?

3. The ratio of sand to cement needed to make mortar is 5:1.

   Ben uses 10 kg of cement.

   How many kgs of sand does he use?

4. Here are four calculations:

     a. $8 - 3 \times 2$ b. $(8 - 3) \times 2$ c. $8 \times 3 \times -2$ d. $8 + 3 \times -2$

   Which of these calculations have the same answer?

5. A new car costs £12 000.

   After one year it has lost 20% of its value.

   What is it worth now?

To get the indented numbers or letters a, b, click the **Increase Indent** icon in the paragraph group and the numbers will automatically change level. To return to the main numbering 1, 2, 3 etc., click the **Decrease Indent** icon.

The options b, c and d in question number 4 have been inserted simply by setting eight tabs and typing the numbers b, c and d together with the text.

If the numbering goes wrong for some reason, you can always restart the numbering from a chosen value (see **Set Numbering value** at the bottom of the screen in **Figure 4.11**.)

Objectives

- ▶ Insert an image into a document
- ▶ Wrap text around an image
- ▶ Group and manipulate images

Inserting an image into a document

Digital photographs, images created using a drawing package and scanned images can all be inserted into Word documents.

- Open the document **Ch 5 Top Cruise destinations with columns.docx** from the **WBTB Exercise documents** folder downloaded from **www.pgonline.co.uk**.

- Open the second document **Ch 5 Top Cruise destinations with images.docx**. You need three images similar to the ones in this document. You can search the Internet for images of Antarctica and an emperor penguin, and save them in your folder. Name them **Antarctica** and **Emperor-penguin**. Close the document when you have found the images you need.

- In **Ch 5 Top Cruise destinations with columns.docx**, insert a blank line after the heading, and centre the cursor using the icon in the **Paragraph** group.

- From the **Insert** ribbon tab, select **Pictures**. In the dialogue box, navigate to the folder containing the saved images and double-click the image **Antarctica.jpg** to insert it.

Pictures

You may need to crop or resize the image to fit.

- Cropping an image will trim it. To crop an image, select the image and click the **Format** tab. Click the **Crop** icon and drag a crop handle. Click the **Crop** icon again to deselect it.

Crop

- To resize an image, drag one of the image handles. Hold **Shift** to constrain the proportions using a corner handle.

Wrapping text

The next two images need different types of text wrapping.

- Insert the image of the penguin underneath the second column. Then right-click it and choose **Size and Position**.

- A dialogue box appears as shown in **Figure 5.1**. Select **Tight**, **Both sides** from the **Text Wrapping** tab.

- Now you can move the penguin up beside the text as shown in **Figure 5.3**.

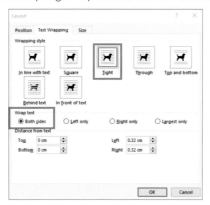

Figure 5.1:
Selecting a
wrapping style

Selecting an online image

Instead of finding an image from the Internet and saving it, you can probably find a suitable image of a cruise ship using Word's **Online Pictures** facility.

- With the cursor on the line below the first column, select **Insert**, **Online pictures**.

- A search box should appear in which you can type a description of the type of image you are looking for. Type **Cruise ship**.

- Select one of the images found and click **Insert**.

- Right-click the image and select **Wrap Text**, **In Front of Text**.

- Drag a corner to resize the image, or crop it as before.

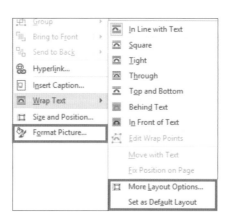

Figure 5.2:
Text wrap options

Your page should look something like **Figure 5.3**.

Three top cruise destinations

Caribbean

Typically you might visit three or four countries on a one-week island-hopping cruise. If you're thinking of a longer trip, you can visit even more islands. Some of the most popular include Jamaica, Barbados, Curaçao, Aruba, St Lucia and St Kitts, with stop-offs to lie on sandy beaches, participate in water sports or take tours to learn about the colourful history of each island.

For a different experience, Cuba is fascinating, and you'll need more than just a one-day stop-off – ships often sail round the island stopping for a day at different ports.

Antarctica

If you fancy a unique cruise to the coldest, most remote part of the earth, Antarctica with its vast, unspoiled landscapes and gigantic icebergs will take your breath away.

You'll cruise on a ship that holds no more than 200 passengers, and disembark to find yourself walking among penguins, getting close to sea lions and buckling on snowshoes for a walk across the spectacular landscape.

Manipulating images

Pictures and other objects may be grouped so that they can then be rotated, flipped, moved or resized as though they were a single object. You can change the attributes of all the objects in the group at the same time, or ungroup them and regroup them later if you need to.

- Open the document **Ch 5 Arizona Canyons.docx** in the **WBTB Exercise documents** folder, downloadable from **www.pgonline.co.uk**. In the document, three images have been copied and pasted below some text. More text appears below the images.

The canyons of Arizona

The Grand Canyon in Arizona is a natural wonder that you simply have to see to believe. Stretching 277 miles from end to end, the steep, rocky walls plunge more than a mile down to the floor of the canyon, where the Colorado river snakes its way towards the Southwest.

Around 5.5 million people visit the Grand Canyon each year. The South Rim can be accessed by free shuttle buses or by personal transport.

Antelope Canyon is a **slot canyon** on Navajo land east of Page, Arizona.

Figure 5.4:
Images in line with text

Selecting several objects

You can usually select several images by holding down the **Ctrl** key while you click each one. However, if you place images using the default **Wrap** option **In Line with Text**, as has been done here, you will find that you cannot select more than one image.

To select several images, you must choose any other **Wrap** option. Try this out as follows:

- Click the first image to select it. A **Layout Options** icon appears beside it.

- Click this icon and in the pop-up window select **In Front of Text**. Alternatively, with the image selected, click **Wrap Text** on the **Format** tab ribbon. Then select **In Front of Text**.

- The second image is now partially hidden. Select it and select the same **Layout** option as before.

- Drag it out of the way so you can see the third image. Select it and set the same **Layout** option.

Note that you can also set **Layout** options by right-clicking the image and selecting **Wrap Text** from the pop-up window, or by choosing **Size and Position**. This enables you to set text wrapping as well as size and position.

Your document will now look something like this:

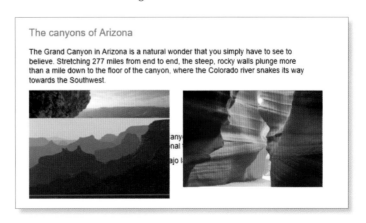

Arranging images

- With the cursor positioned at the end of the first block of text, press **Enter** several times so that the second block of text appears below the images.

- Drag the images so that the lower edges of the three images are lined up, overlapping each other.

- Click the first image. On the **Format** tab ribbon, click **Bring Forward** in the **Arrange** group.

Cropping an image

The third image has a greater vertical height than the other two, and needs to be cropped.

- Select the image and click **Crop** in the **Size** group on the **Format** tab ribbon.

- Drag the crop handle in the centre at the top of the image down, to make it the same height as the other two images.

- Click the **Crop** icon again to deselect it.

Figure 5.7:
Images lined up
horizontally

Rotating images

You can arrange the three images in a fan by rotating them.

- With the first image selected, grab the **Rotate** handle at the centre top of the image and drag left. The image rotates.

- Rotate the third image clockwise. Adjust horizontal and vertical positioning.

Figure 5.8:
Fan of images

Grouping images

- Hold down the **Ctrl** key while you select each image in turn. On the **Layout** ribbon, select **Group** .

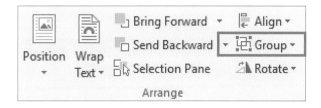

Figure 5.9:
The Arrange group

Now you can size or format the whole group together.

- Click the group of images and make it smaller by dragging a corner handle. (Keep the **Shift** key pressed to maintain its proportions, and the **Ctrl** key pressed to keep it centred.)

- Right-click the group and choose **Format Object**... from the bottom of the pop-up window.

- The **Format Picture** options will be displayed on the right of the screen. Try the effect of some of the options. **Shadow** has been selected below.

The effect of the options selected in **Figure 5.10** is shown in **Figure 5.11**.

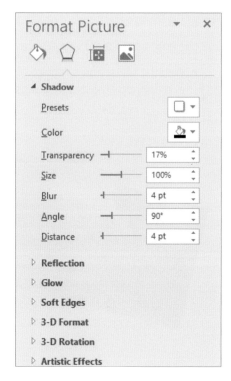

Figure 5.10:
Formatting a group of objects

Figure 5.11:
Shadows added to all images in the group

42

Objectives

▶ Insert and manipulate shapes

▶ Group and ungroup shapes

▶ Use the drawing canvas

Figure 6.1:
Shapes Gallery

Inserting a shape into a document

To insert a ready-made shape such as a circle, square or arrow, click the **Insert** tab and select **Shapes** in the **Illustrations** group on the ribbon.

A pop-up window shows the different shapes available (Figure 6.1).

● Click a shape and then click in your document where you want it inserted.

● Drag a side or corner handle to make it the required size.

● Drag an edge to position the shape more precisely. To centre the shape between left and right margins, drag it horizontally and a vertical green guide line appears as the centre handles of the shape move across the centre of the page.

After you have inserted a shape, the **Format** tab appears whenever the shape is selected. Using icons on the **Format** ribbon you can insert, edit and manipulate shapes and text within shapes.

43

Manipulating and formatting a shape

Constraining a shape

To create a perfect square or circle (or to constrain the dimensions of other shapes), press and hold **Shift** while you drag when creating the shape.

When creating a straight line, holding down **Shift** ensures that the line is vertical or horizontal.

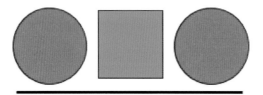

Figure 6.2:
Constraining a shape

Making an existing line horizontal or vertical

Sometimes you may have an existing line that is slightly out of the desired horizontal or vertical position.

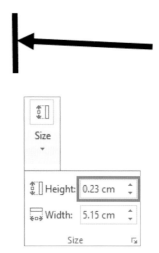

Figure 6.3:
Making a line horizontal

To make sure a line is horizontal, for example, click to select it and then on the **Format** ribbon, set the **Height** to zero in the **Size** panel. This will make the line horizontal. Setting **Width** to zero for a near vertical line will make the line vertical.

Copying a shape

Method 1:   Right-click the shape and from the pop-up menu, select **Copy**. Right-click again and select **Paste Options**. Choose the left-hand **Paste** icon. Then drag the copy to where you want it.

Method 2:   On the **Home** tab in the **Clipboard** group, use the **Copy** and **Paste** icons.

Method 3:   Press and hold **Ctrl** while you drag the shape to a new location. To constrain the position and alignment of the copied shape horizontally or vertically, press and hold both **Ctrl** and **Shift** while you drag a shape.

Rotating or flipping a shape

You can rotate a shape or image by selecting it and dragging the **Rotate** handle left or right. For more exact rotations, or to flip a shape horizontally or vertically, in the **Arrange** group on the **Format** ribbon click the **Rotate** icon.

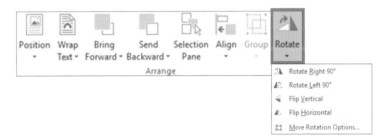

Figure 6.4:
Rotate icon in the
Format ribbon

Grouping and ungrouping shapes

Select several shapes by holding down **Ctrl** while you select each one. Then in the **Arrange** group on the **Format** ribbon click the **Group** icon or press **Ctrl + G**.

A selection box will appear around all the shapes. You can then drag the surrounding border and all the shapes inside it will be moved together. By dragging on one of the side handles, you can distort the shapes. Dragging on any of the corner handles lets you change the size of all the objects in the group.

To ungroup the shapes, on the **Format** tab, select **Arrange**, **Group**, **Ungroup** or **Ctrl + Shift + G**.

Figure 6.5:
Grouped shapes

The drawing canvas

At the bottom of the **Shapes** options box is the **New Drawing Canvas** icon. If you need to create several shapes, such as the ones used in the sailboat shown in **Figure 6.5**, or a flowchart, for example, it is advisable to first select **New Drawing Canvas**. The purpose of the drawing canvas is to provide a container for all the individual shapes that make up your image so that you can move or size them altogether. It is initially transparent and has no border round it.

A further advantage of using a drawing canvas is that you can "lasso" all the objects inside the canvas to group them, rather than selecting them individually.

Drawing a flowchart

A flowchart is used in this exercise as an example of a diagram which has several shapes which need to be lined up and have text inserted into them. The flowchart used in this example shows an algorithm or procedure for calculating the points scored in a football league, depending on whether the match was won, drawn or lost. The flowchart to be drawn is shown at the end of the chapter in **Figure 6.14**.

1. If you want your flowchart centred horizontally, start by clicking the **Centre** icon in the **Paragraph** group on the **Home** tab.

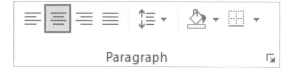

Figure 6.6:
Paragraph group

2. Select **Insert**, **Shapes** and select **New Drawing canvas**.

3. Select **Insert**, **Shapes** and select the **Terminator** symbol from the **Flowchart** group. Insert a shape at the top of the drawing canvas. It should be large enough to insert some text. It may look something like this:

4. There are several default **Shape Styles** options to choose from, which you can click to see the effect. If none of them is quite what you want, you can customise the format.

Figure 6.7:
Shape Styles options
on Format ribbon tab

5. At this stage it is important to select a shape with black text. Then select the **Format** tab and set **Shape Fill** to **White**, **Shape Outline** to **Black**. You can experiment with changing the line weight.

Adding text to a shape

6. Right-click your shape and select **Add text** from the shortcut menu.

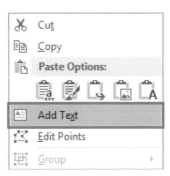

Figure 6.8:
Adding text to a shape

7. Type **Start** in the box. If nothing appears, it is probably because, when placing your shape, you chose a format with white text instead of black. To change it to black, select the invisible text and on the **Format** tab, select the **Text Fill** icon. Select **Black** (**Figure 6.9**).

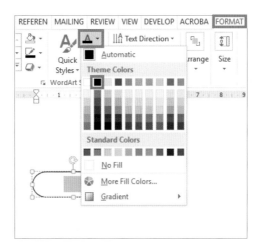

Figure 6.9:
Selecting a Text
Fill colour

You can select the text and change its font, size, alignment or paragraph spacing from the **Home** tab.

Formatting text in a shape

8. You should now have the first flowchart box with its text inserted. Set the font to **Arial** and the font size to **9pt**. The next flowchart box to be inserted has more text in it than will fit.

9. Insert a diamond-shaped flowchart box under the Start box. Then select **Add text**, as before, and type "Match won?" Even after reducing the font size to 9pt, it may not quite fit in the box. This is because by default, the text has margins around it. These need to be reset.

10. Select the diamond shaped (decision) box and right-click its border. Select **Format Shape**… from the bottom of the pop-up menu. A **Format Shape** options box will appear on the right of the document. Select **Text Options**. Select the **Layout** and **Properties** icon.

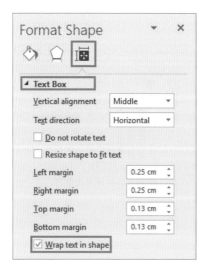

Figure 6.10:
Formatting a shape

11. Set left, right, top and bottom margins to zero. Make sure **Wrap text in shape** is selected.

12. Check and adjust the **Paragraph** settings if the text is not centred in the box.

Changing default settings for a shape

All the flowchart boxes need to have a white fill and a black outline, so it will save time to change the **Default Shape** settings before drawing any more shapes. Note that changing the default will apply only to the document that is currently open. To set defaults for all documents you would have to create a new template.

13. With the shape selected, right-click the border and then click **Set as Default Shape** on the shortcut menu.

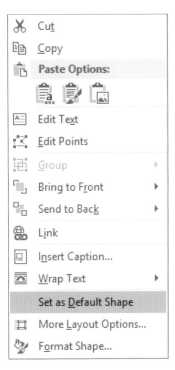

Figure 6.11:
Shortcut menu

Inserting more flowchart boxes

Now you can create new boxes as shown below, using copy and paste where this saves time, and editing the text. The boxes may not be very well lined up and there are no lines connecting the boxes yet. This will be fixed in a minute. So far, you should have something like this:

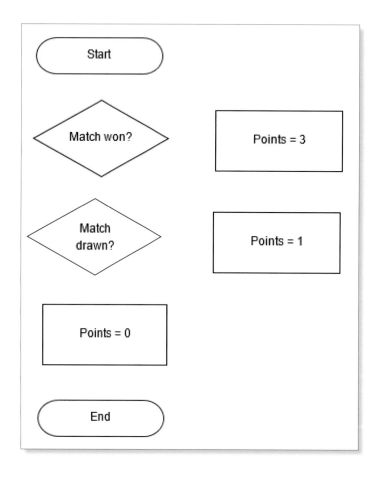

Aligning objects

To align all the flowchart boxes vertically, drag across ("lasso") them inside the Drawing Canvas to select all the boxes down the left-hand side. Then select **Align, Align Center** in the **Arrange** group on the **Format** tab.

To align two boxes horizontally, select them and then click **Arrange, Align, Align middle**.

You can make the spacing between each box equal by selecting **Align, Distribute Vertically**. The boxes will line themselves up neatly as in the final flowchart shown in **Figure 6.14**.

Sending objects to front or back

It remains to draw lines connecting the boxes. To draw a horizontal or vertical line, hold down **Shift** while you draw the line. Use the arrow keys to nudge a line up, down, left or right.

To copy a line (or any other shape) so that it appears directly below the shape being copied, hold down **Shift** and **Ctrl** together while you drag the line.

1. On the **Insert** tab, select **Shapes** and select the **Line** symbol. Draw a line from the Start box to the End box. Hold down **Shift** while you draw the line to make sure it is vertical. It will be placed in front of all the boxes.

2. Select the line and in the **Arrange** group on the **Format** tab select **Send Backward**, **Send to Back**. If it is still visible in front of the flowchart boxes, this may be because the boxes are transparent (have no fill) rather than having a white fill. You need to select the flowchart boxes and give each of them a white fill.

3. Add the other lines to the flowchart, as in **Figure 6.14**.

4. Format the lines that require arrows by selecting them and using the **Shape Outline** icon on the **Format** tab. Once you have formatted one line with an arrow, you can select others and use **Ctrl-Y** to format them in the same way.

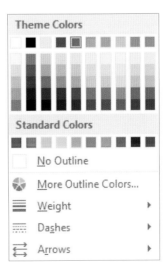

Figure 6.13:
Format line

5. To insert the labels "Yes" and "No" on the flowchart, on the **Format** tab select **Shapes** and choose **Text Box**. Draw a small text box, insert "Yes", format it with no border or fill and place it on the flowchart. Copy, paste and amend it to create the other text boxes.

The completed flowchart

Here it is!

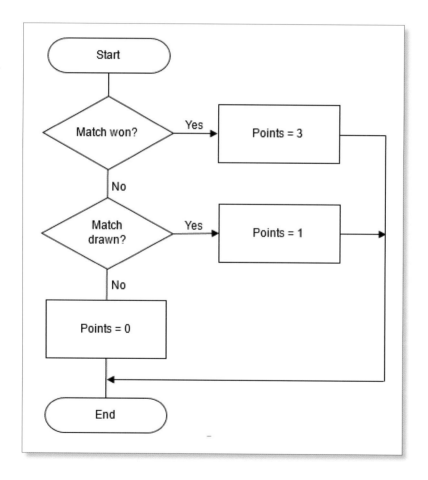

Figure 6.14:
The completed
flowchart

Chapter 7 Tables

Objectives

- Insert a table of several columns into a document
- Format a table

Why use tables?

Tables are useful in any situation where data needs to be laid out neatly in rows and columns, for example tables of currency or weight conversions, maximum and minimum temperatures in different months or times of film showings at a cinema.

The table below shows the opening times of a garden and woodland which the public can visit.

		M	T	W	T	F	S	S
Garden, shop and tea-room								
29 Mar – 31 May	12-5*		**T**	**W**	**T**			
1 Jun – 31 Aug	12-5*		**T**	**W**	**T**			**S**
1 Sep – 27 Oct	12-5*		**T**	**W**	**T**			
Woodland trail								
1 Mar – 30 Oct	11-5:30		**T**	**W**	**T**		**S**	**S**
*House opens at 1pm. Also open Good Friday and Easter Sunday, Sundays 1 and 29 May and Bank Holiday Mondays								

Figure 7.1:
A sample table

Inserting a table into a document

To insert a new table at the current cursor position in a document, click the **Insert** tab and then click the down-arrow under **Table** in the **Tables** group near the left-hand end of the ribbon.

There are two easy methods of inserting a table.

The completed table has nine columns and eight rows, so you could insert it by dragging across the appropriate number of columns and rows and then clicking the mouse button:

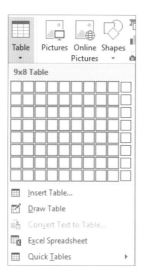

Figure 7.2:
Quick way of
entering a table

This method inserts a table with cells of a default fixed size, typically 1cm wide and 0.45cm high, and is suitable for inserting many simple tables. Cell size can easily be changed.

The second method is to click **Insert Table…** which gives you more options.

Figure 7.3:
Specifying properties
for a new table

This time, use the second method to create the table.

- Open a new document.

- On the **Insert** tab select **Table, Insert Table**… and specify 9 columns and 8 rows.

- Click **AutoFit to contents**. This will cause the cell width to widen automatically as you type, if the column width is too narrow. A small table will appear, with nine columns and eight rows.

Entering text in the table

- In the first row, starting in column 3, enter **M, T, W, T, F, S, S** in consecutive columns, for the days of the week.

- In the third row, enter text as shown in **Figure 7.4**. Tab to get to the next cell in a row. (If you enter data in the wrong cell, select and drag it to where it should be.)

		M	T	W	T	F	S	S
29 Mar – 31 May	12-5*		T	W	T			
1 Jun – 31 Aug								
1 Sep – 27 Oct								
1 Mar – 30 Oct								

Figure 7.4:
Entering text in
the table

Copying and pasting text in the table

- Copy the text **12-5*** and **T W T** in row 3 by selecting the five cells and pressing **Ctrl-C**.

- Paste the text into the two rows beneath by dragging across the 10 cells and pressing **Ctrl-V**.

- Enter the text in row 7 for opening days and times between **1 Mar – 30 Oct**.

- Insert the other text for Saturday and Sunday as shown in **Figure 7.5**.

		M	T	W	T	F	S	S
29 Mar – 31 May	12-5*		T	W	T			
1 Jun – 31 Aug	12-5*		T	W	T			S
1 Sep – 27 Oct	12-5*		T	W	T			
1 Mar – 30 Oct	11-5:30		T	W	T		S	S

Figure 7.5:
Copying and
pasting text

The Layout tab ribbon

There are two **Layout** tabs. The table **Layout** tab is visible only when a table is selected, or the cursor is currently in a cell of a table. Click it, and the **Layout** ribbon appears as shown in **Figure 7.6**.

Figure 7.6:
The Layout ribbon

Adding and deleting rows and columns

Using buttons in the **Rows and columns** group, you can add and delete rows and columns.

- To insert a row above or below the current cursor position in a table, click **Insert Above** or **Insert Below**.

- To insert multiple rows, drag the cursor down to highlight at least one cell in as many rows as you want to insert. Then click **Insert Above** or **Insert Below**.

- To delete rows, drag the cursor down to highlight at least one cell in as many rows as you want to delete. Then click **Delete**.

The procedure for inserting and deleting columns is similar.

Merging cells

The text in rows 2, 6 and 8 of the sample table in **Figure 7.1** goes right across the table. The cells in each of these rows needs to be merged into a single cell.

- Click anywhere in the table to make the **Layout** tab visible.

- Drag across all the cells in the second row. This will cause the greyed-out **Merge Cells** button to become active.

- Click **Merge cells**.

- Repeat this operation by dragging across the cells in Row 6 and either clicking the **Merge Cells** button again or by pressing **Ctrl-Y** to repeat the last operation. Do the same in Row 8.

- Now type the text in rows 2, 6 and 8 as shown in **Figure 7.7**.

		M	T	W	T	F	S	S
Garden, shop and tea-room								
29 Mar – 31 May	12-5*		T	W	T			
1 Jun – 31 Aug	12-5*		T	W	T			S
1 Sep – 27 Oct	12-5*		T	W	T			
Woodland trail								
1 Mar – 30 Oct	11-5:30		T	W	T		S	S
*House opens at 1pm. Also open Good Friday and Easter Sunday, Sundays 1 and 29 May and Bank Holiday Mondays								

Figure 7.7:
Merging cells

Inserting a soft line break

Notice that because we chose **AutoFit to contents**, the cell in the last row continues to widen as you enter text until the table occupies the full width of the document, when it automatically wraps. To prevent this, you can insert a **soft line break** at any point in the text.

- Click where you want to break the line.

- Press **Shift-Enter**. Alternatively, click the **Layout** tab next to the **References** tab, and on the ribbon, click **Breaks, Text Wrapping**.

Selecting and emboldening cells

- Highlight the text in row 2, and press and hold down the **Ctrl** key while you drag across all the cells containing the first letter of each day (M, T, W etc.) in rows 3 to 7.

- Click **Ctrl-B** to make all these cells bold.

		M	T	W	T	F	S	S
Garden, shop and tea-room								
29 Mar – 31 May	12-5*		**T**	**W**	**T**			
1 Jun – 31 Aug	12-5*		**T**	**W**	**T**			**S**
1 Sep – 27 Oct	12-5*		**T**	**W**	**T**			
Woodland trail								
1 Mar – 30 Oct	11-5:30		**T**	**W**	**T**		**S**	**S**
*House opens at 1pm. Also open Good Friday and Easter Sunday, Sundays 1 and 29 May and Bank Holiday Mondays								

Figure 7.8:
Soft line breaks
and bold text

Changing cell dimensions and layout

Cell dimensions, alignment and text orientation can be changed using buttons on the table **Layout** ribbon.

Figure 7.9:
Changing cell
dimensions and layout

Changing column width or row height

You can specify the width of individual columns or of a whole table, using options in the **Cell Size** group. Select cells in the columns you want to change, and then either type in a dimension such as **1 cm** or click the up- or down-arrows on the buttons to incrementally increase or decrease column width.

Changing row height

- To change the row height in every row, select the table by clicking in the table and then clicking the icon at the top left corner. In the **Layout** ribbon, click the up-arrow in the **Cell Size** group to increase the row height, or just type the value that you want, for example **1 cm**. Press **Enter**.

- Drag the bottom border of the last row downwards to increase the row height of this cell.

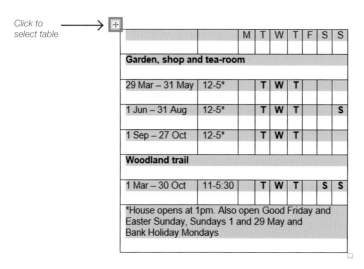

Figure 7.10:
Increasing row height

Changing text alignment

Now that the rows are deeper, it becomes apparent that the text is hugging the top of each row. It would look better if the text was vertically centred.

- Select the table and click the left-hand, middle row button in the **Alignment** group on the **Layout** ribbon, which makes the text left-aligned and vertically centred.

Figure 7.11:
Cell size and
Alignment groups

- You can separately align cells containing days of the week to the centre of their respective cells. The cells are so narrow that you may not notice any difference.

		M	T	W	T	F	S	S
Garden, shop and tea-room								
29 Mar – 31 May	12-5*		T	W	T			
1 Jun – 31 Aug	12-5*		T	W	T			S
1 Sep – 27 Oct	12-5*		T	W	T			
Woodland trail								
1 Mar – 30 Oct	11-5:30		T	W	T		S	S
*House opens at 1pm. Also open Good Friday and Easter Sunday, Sundays 1 and 29 May and Bank Holiday Mondays								

Figure 7.12:
Left aligned, vertically
centred text

Problems with text alignment

Sometimes text may not appear to be vertically centred even when this has been specified. If that happens, highlight the affected cells and on the **Home** ribbon, click the down-arrow in the **Paragraph** group and check line and paragraph spacing. **Line spacing** should be set to **Single** and **Spacing Before** and **After** to **0**.

Customising borders

Borders can be added or removed by clicking the **Borders** icon on the **Home** ribbon and selecting options from the pop-up window.

Figure 7.13:
Border options

- Select all the text in the table and click the **Inside Vertical Border** option to deselect it.

The inside vertical borders will disappear from the table. Gridlines can be toggled on or off using the **View Gridlines** option in the **Borders** pop-up window.

	M T W T F S S
Garden, shop and tea-room	
29 Mar – 31 May 12-5*	T W T
1 Jun – 31 Aug 12-5*	T W T S
1 Sep – 27 Oct 12-5*	T W T
Woodland trail	
1 Mar – 30 Oct 11-5:30	T W T S S
*House opens at 1pm. Also open Good Friday and Easter Sunday, Sundays 1 and 29 May and Bank Holiday Mondays	

Figure 7.14:
Removing inside
vertical borders

Border painter

The horizontal borders on either side of rows 2 and 6 can be made thicker using options on the **Design** tab ribbon.

Figure 7.15:
Border Painter on
the Design ribbon

- Click the cursor in the second row of the table, which is a single merged cell.
- Click the down-arrow in the bottom right-hand corner of the **Border Painter** button.
- A dialogue box opens.
- Set the options as shown in **Figure 7.16**. To do this select the colour **Blue**, a line width of **2 ¼ pt**, and then click the top and bottom borders of the large image in the centre of the right-hand **Preview**. Change the **Apply to:** box to **Cell**, and click **OK**.

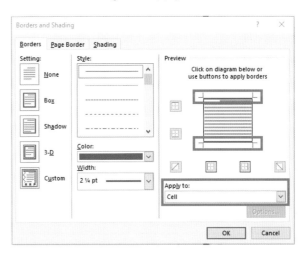

Figure 7.16:
Borders and Shading
dialogue box

- To apply the same borders to line 6, click in row 6 and press **Ctrl-Y** to repeat the formatting. Alternatively, just go through the same steps again.

Applying shading

- With the cursor in the bottom row, click the down-arrow in the bottom right-hand corner of the **Border Painter** button.

- Click the **Shading** tab in the dialogue box.

- Set the options for the cell as shown in **Figure 7.17**.

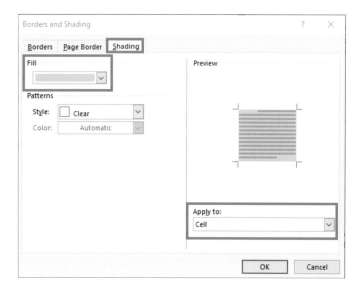

Figure 7.17:
Applying shading

Your completed table now looks like this:

	M T W T F S S
Garden, shop and tea-room	
29 Mar – 31 May 12-5*	T W T
1 Jun – 31 Aug 12-5*	T W T S
1 Sep – 27 Oct 12-5*	T W T
Woodland trail	
1 Mar – 30 Oct 11-5:30	T W T S S
*House opens at 1pm. Also open Good Friday and Easter Sunday, Sundays 1 and 29 May and Bank Holiday Mondays	

Figure 7.18:
The completed table

Objectives

▶ Use the numeric keypad

▶ Enter symbols and special characters

▶ Use the equation editor

The numeric keypad

Most keyboards supplied with a PC have a numeric keypad at the right-hand end. This is convenient for entering data consisting entirely of numbers.

When you switch on your computer, by default the **Num Lock** key, located above the numeric keypad, is normally ON. This is indicated by the leftmost light at the top of the keyboard.

In the same way as the **Caps Lock** key turns all letters into uppercase, the **Num Lock** key switches on or off the secondary function of the keys on the numeric keypad. In order to use the **Alt** key combinations described in this chapter, the **Num Lock** key must be ON.

(Note that on a laptop, once you have turned on **Num Lock**, the numeric keys are 7, 8, 9, U, I, O, J, K, L and M. These correspond to 7, 8, 9, 4, 5, 6, 1, 2, 3, 0).)

Num Lock, Caps Lock and Scroll Lock indicator lights

Alt key

Figure 8.1:
A standard keyboard

Typing accents

Commonly accented letters as used in many foreign languages can be typed by holding down the **Alt** key while typing the appropriate number combination using the numeric keypad. Alternatively they can be inserted by typing a **Ctrl** key combination followed by the letter that needs the accent. Here are some examples:

	Alt key	Ctrl key	Comment /Further guidance	Example
é	**Alt** + 130	**Ctrl** + '	**Ctrl** + single quote mark followed by **e**	café
â	**Alt** + 131	**Ctrl** + ^	**Ctrl** + **Shift** + 6 followed by **a**	gâteau
à	**Alt** + 133	**Ctrl** + `	**Ctrl** + back tick (under Esc key) followed by **a**	à la carte
ç	**Alt** + 135	**Ctrl** + ,	**Ctrl** + comma followed by **c**	François
ê	**Alt** + 136	**Ctrl** + ^	**Ctrl** + **Shift** + 6 followed by **e**	fête
è	**Alt** + 138	**Ctrl** + `	**Ctrl** + back tick (under Esc key) followed by **e**	crèche
ö	**Alt** + 148	**Ctrl** + :	**Ctrl** + **Shift** + : followed by **o**	Nöel

For example, to type **à**, hold down **Alt** while you type **133**, or alternatively, hold down **Ctrl** while you type a back-tick character (located under the **Esc** key), and then type **a**.

The **AltGr** (**Gr**aph) key to the right of the Space bar is seldom used but one useful key combination is **AltGr-4** which produces the Euro currency symbol **€**. (The **€** symbol commonly appears on the keyboard key **4**.)

Inserting symbols

To insert symbols such as mathematical symbols or tick boxes, click the **Insert** tab and on the ribbon, click the **Symbol** button and then **Symbol**, **More Symbols**… A dialogue box will open:

Figure 8.2:
Symbol dialogue box

You can choose from numerous different fonts. The font in **Figure 8.2** shows some of the symbols that you will see if you select **Symbol** font. Symbols that you have used recently appear in the window and you can click any of these to select them. Then click **Insert** followed by **Close**.

Inserting special characters

To insert a character such as ©, ® or ™, click the **Insert** tab and on the ribbon, click the **Symbol** button and then **Symbol**, **More Symbols**… The dialogue box shown in **Figure 8.2** will open. Clicking the **Special characters** tab at the top of the window will display various symbols such as ©, ®, ™ and other characters. If you use any of these frequently, it is worth remembering the shortcut key combination for it, for example **Ctrl-Alt-R** for ®.

Autocorrect options

Word automatically corrects common spelling mistakes like "teh" instead of "the", as you type. Some of these automatic corrections can be annoying – for example you may not want (c) to be automatically replaced by the copyright symbol ©. You can undo the automatic correction by pressing the **Undo** button on the Quick Access Toolbar or by pressing **Crtl-Z** (the shortcut key combination for **Undo**) as soon as the symbol appears.

To change **AutoCorrect** options, click the **AutoCorrect**… button at the bottom of the **Symbol** dialogue box (**Figure 8.2**) and change any of the options.

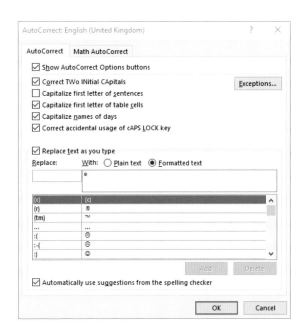

Figure 8.3:
AutoCorrect options

Using the equation editor

If you need to write sentences containing fractions, or mathematical symbols of all kinds, you can do this using the **Equation Editor**. For example, suppose you want to write the following sentence:

- Click in the sentence where you want to insert a fraction.

- Click the **Insert** tab and on the ribbon, select **Equation**. If **Equation** is not visible, click **Symbols** and then **Equation**.

- The **Design** ribbon will appear. If your open window is narrow, the **Structures** group may be collapsed and not visible. In that case, click the down-arrow underneath **Structures** or widen the window.

![The Equation Design ribbon]

Figure 8.4
The Equation
Design ribbon

- In your document, a space will appear for you to type your equation (or fraction in this case). A shortcut is **Alt + =**.

![A kilometre is approximate Type equation here.]

Figure 8.5:
Inserting an equation

- Click the down-arrow in the **Fraction** group.

- Options appear:

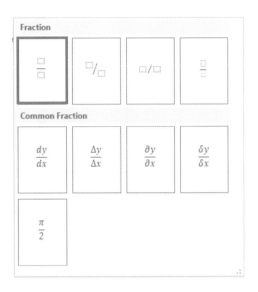

- Click the first option and in the numerator (top) of the fraction type 5. In the denominator (bottom) of the fraction, type 8.

A kilometre is approximately $\frac{5}{8}$

- Click outside the equation and continue.

- Using different equation, formula and fraction formats, you can construct complex equations, for example:

$$\frac{a^2}{\sqrt[3]{27}} = 12$$

Inserting accents or overbars

{()} Bracket ▾

sinθ Function ▾

ä Accent ▾

If you want to type an expression with an overbar, for example $\overline{A+B}$, you need a combination of **Equation** and **Accent**.

- On the **Insert** ribbon, choose **Equation**, **Insert New Equation**.

- Click the down-arrow next to the *ä* **Accent** icon.

A pop-up window appears showing different types of accents, overbars and underbars:

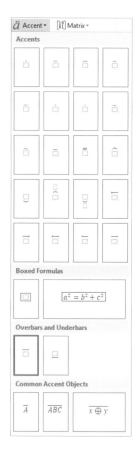

Figure 8.8:
Inserting an overbar

- Select the first symbol in the **Overbars and Underbars** group (**Figure 8.8**).

- Type A + B in the equation box:

Type equation here.

Figure 8.9:
Equation box

- Click outside the equation box to continue with text.

Note that expressions created using this method use the **Cambria Math** font. You can make the text bigger or smaller, but you cannot change the font.

Chapter 9
Long documents

Objectives

▶ Use and edit styles

▶ Create a Table of Contents

▶ Create section breaks with customised headers and footers

Formatting a document

There are hundreds of different types of document, including reports written for a school project, scientific studies, magazines and so on. Although they may each vary in format, many have certain elements in common:

● title page

● Table of Contents

● several parts, chapters or sections, which may be numbered, each typically starting on a new page

● subsections, which may be numbered.

A document may be formatted in Word using default or customised styles for each section and subsection. When the report is written using styles, a Table of Contents can be automatically created at the front of the document.

In this chapter you will learn how to format a multi-page document with a title page, preface and five chapters, each containing several sections. You will then add a Table of Contents after the preface, and add different headers and footers for the Preface and each chapter.

Open the eleven-page document named **Ch 9 Flying Machines 1912 extracts** which is in the folder **WBTB exercise documents** downloadable from the website **www.pgonline.co.uk**. This contains extracts from a much longer document published in 1912. The document contains very little formatting and uses no predefined styles, and you can use it to practise the Word skills described.

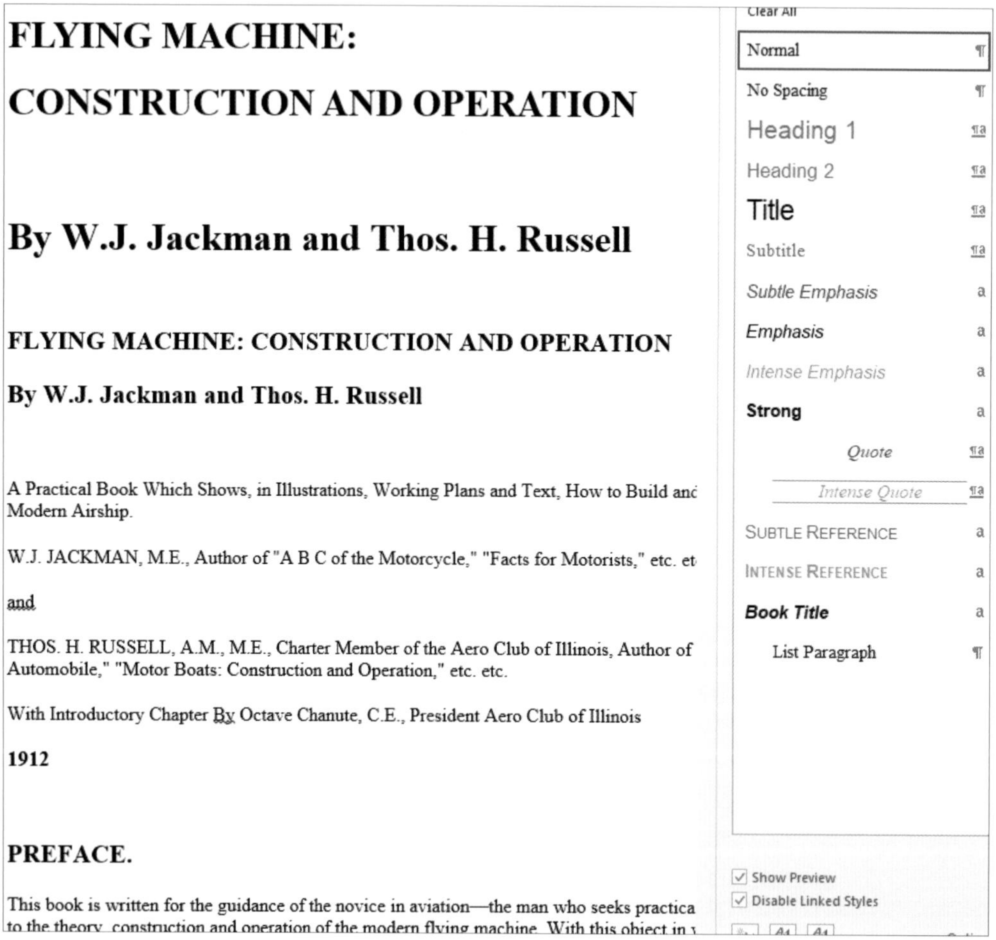

FLYING MACHINE:

CONSTRUCTION AND OPERATION

By W.J. Jackman and Thos. H. Russell

FLYING MACHINE: CONSTRUCTION AND OPERATION

By W.J. Jackman and Thos. H. Russell

A Practical Book Which Shows, in Illustrations, Working Plans and Text, How to Build and Modern Airship.

W.J. JACKMAN, M.E., Author of "A B C of the Motorcycle," "Facts for Motorists," etc. et

and

THOS. H. RUSSELL, A.M., M.E., Charter Member of the Aero Club of Illinois, Author of Automobile," "Motor Boats: Construction and Operation," etc. etc.

With Introductory Chapter By Octave Chanute, C.E., President Aero Club of Illinois

1912

PREFACE.

This book is written for the guidance of the novice in aviation—the man who seeks practica to the theory, construction and operation of the modern flying machine. With this object in y

Styles pane	
Clear All	
Normal	¶
No Spacing	¶
Heading 1	¶a
Heading 2	¶a
Title	¶a
Subtitle	¶a
Subtle Emphasis	a
Emphasis	a
Intense Emphasis	a
Strong	a
Quote	¶a
Intense Quote	¶a
SUBTLE REFERENCE	a
INTENSE REFERENCE	a
Book Title	a
List Paragraph	¶

☑ Show Preview
☑ Disable Linked Styles

Figure 9.1:
The first page of the sample document

Setting font styles for the document

The title page

Make sure you have the inbuilt styles showing, by clicking the down-arrow at the corner of the **Styles** group on the **Home** ribbon. The **Styles** pane is displayed showing built-in styles called **Title** and **Subtitle**, which you could use for the title and authors' names.

- Experiment with fonts and size for the title.

- When you are happy with the style, right-click the **Title** style and select **Update Heading 1 style to match selection**.

- Choose a font and size for the authors' names, and update the **Subtitle** style to match it.

Inserting page breaks

- Place your cursor at the start of the line where the title is repeated, and press **Ctrl-Enter** to insert a page break. The next page gives some information about the authors and the book (so-called "front matter").

- Insert more page breaks before the titles **Preface**, **Contents** and **Chapter 1**.

- Insert page breaks between each chapter.

Chapter headings and sub-headings

First you need to choose a style for the chapter headings. You can stick with the style currently used in the document, go with the default **Heading 1** style, or design a style of your own. The document is more than 100 years old so something fairly old-fashioned will look quite appropriate. You could increase the font size too.

- Select the **Chapter 1** heading and increase the font size to **24**. Right-click **Heading 1** in the **Styles** pane and select **Update Heading 1 to Match Selection**.

- Select the first paragraph of text and change the font and paragraph spacing if you want to. Then right-click **Normal** in the **Styles** pane and update the style to match your selected text. All the main text in the document will automatically update to your new style.

- Now adjust the font for the sub-headings, "Second Wenham Aeroplane", "Experiments by Stringfellow", etc. To do this, select one of these section headings, increase the font size and make it bold. Right-click the **Heading 2** style and update it to match the selection.

Update styles throughout the document

You need to update the style of the sub-headings throughout the document, since they are all **Normal** style in the original document. You may find this is quicker if you make the document window full screen and reduce the page size so that you can view two or more pages on the screen at once. (Use the Zoom bar at the bottom right of the document's Status Bar.)

- Click in the margin beside each sub-heading while holding down the **Ctrl** key, thus selecting several of them. Then click **Heading 2** in the **Styles** pane.

- Follow the same procedure to set all the **Chapter** headings to **Heading 1** style.

Creating a Table of Contents

If you have used Styles, creating a Table of Contents and updating it if you amend or add to the document, is very quick.

- Select the heading **Contents** and make it a similar font and size to the section headings. Do not give it a built-in style or it will appear as an entry in the **Table of Contents**.

- Position the cursor underneath the heading **Contents** near the front of the document.

- Under the **References** tab, select **Table of Contents** at the left-hand end of the ribbon.

A dialogue box opens from which you can select a format:

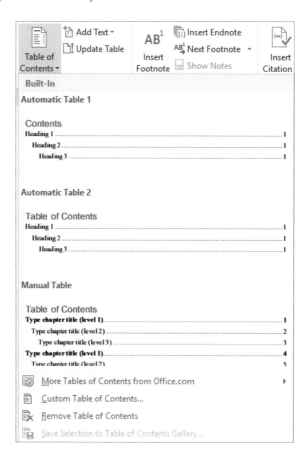

Figure 9.2:
Built in styles for
Table of Contents

- Choose the first or second option.

Hey presto! The Table of Contents appears as shown in **Figure 9.3**. However, you have not yet added page numbers to each page of the document – this will be done shortly.

Figure 9.3:
The Table of Contents

- Delete the extra unwanted blue heading **Contents**.

Creating a customised Table of Contents

If you have different styles in your document, called something other than **Heading 1** and **Heading 2**, or you want a different layout or font, you can click the down-arrow and select **Custom Table of Contents**. This gives you the chance to change the styles that define what goes into the table, the font, whether the table is to have leader dots, and so on.

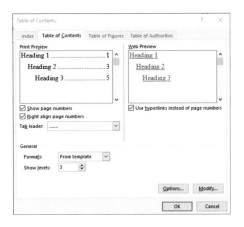

Figure 9.4:
Customising the
Table of Contents

Updating a Table of Contents (TOC)

You should not make any manual changes to the TOC, since if you update it as described below, these changes will be lost. However, if you add extra sections, or make any changes to the main text which affect pagination, you will need to update the TOC. Clicking in the TOC will cause an **Update Table** icon to appear at the top:

Figure 9.5:
Updating the Table
of Contents

- Click the icon and you will have a choice of just updating page numbers, or updating the whole table.

- The shortcut key for updating the table is **F9**.

Adding section breaks

You can open a version of the document called **Ch 9 Flying machines with styles and contents.docx** which has been completed up to this point, if you have not created your own version. You need to add page numbers at the bottom (or top) of each page, and you will also add the Chapter number and title. However, neither of these should appear on the title page. The Acknowledgements and Preface could have page numbers ii and iii, and Chapter 1 will start on page number 1. (In a book, note that odd page numbers are always on the right-hand page.)

You need to add section breaks wherever the header or footer is to change – in this case, at the end of the first, second and third pages and again at the end of every chapter.

- Position the cursor at the start of the second page.

- On the **Layout** ribbon, select **Breaks**. Under **Section Breaks**, select **Next Page**.

Figure 9.6:
Inserting a
section break

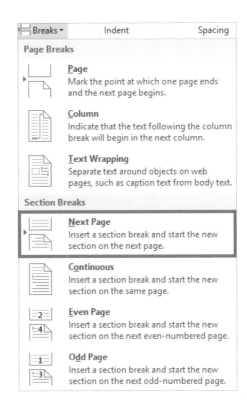

A blank page may appear before the preface. To see why, click the paragraph ¶ symbol on the **Home** ribbon to display the non-printing characters. You have already inserted a page break, and now you have added a section break which also incorporates a page break.

- Delete the page break by double-clicking it and pressing the **Delete** key.

- Delete page breaks and insert section breaks before each chapter heading.

Figure 9.7:
Displaying
non-printing
characters

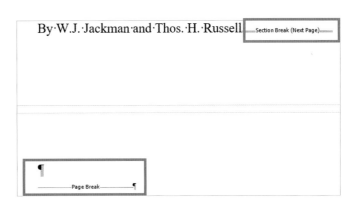

Headers and footers

Any text or graphic placed in the header or footer area of the page (i.e. the top or the bottom, outside the margins of the text) will appear on every page of the document. If the document is divided into more than one section, a different header and/or footer may be placed in each section.

A header is useful in a long document to tell a reader what chapter or section they are currently looking at. It can also be useful in a school project, for example, to identify the title and author. In an advertising brochure, the company name, phone number and website address may be shown in the header or footer.

Page numbers may be placed either in the header or the footer section.

Adding text to a header or footer

Double-click in the footer section at the bottom of the second page to reveal the footer. You will see that this is Section 2.

Figure 9.8:
Section 2 footer

This footer will not be the same as the footer in the previous section, since it will have a page number. To change the default **Same as Previous**, click the **Link to Previous** icon in the **Navigation** group to deselect it. The label **Same as Previous** should disappear from the footer.

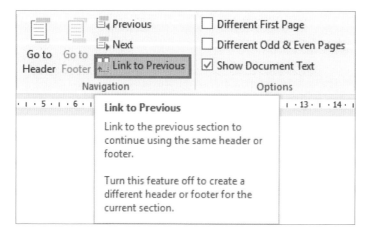

Figure 9.9:
Breaking link to previous footer

- Press the **Tab** key to move to the default tab position in the middle of the footer, click **Page Number** in the **Header and Footer** Group on the ribbon and select **Current Position**.

- Click **Page Number** a second time and select **Format Page Numbers**… Enter the settings as shown in **Figure 9.10**.

Figure 9.10:
Formatting
page number

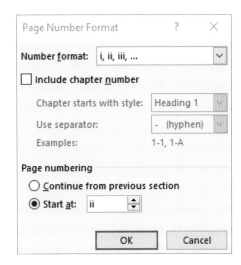

Move to the bottom of Page 5, which is first page of Chapter 1.

- Break the **Link to Previous** as before.

- Click **Page Number** and select **Format Page Numbers**… Amend **Start at** to start at Page 1.

- All the other chapters will have page numbers which follow on automatically from the current section if you leave **Same as Previous** in the rest of the Section footers.

Inserting headers

Customised headers in each section are created in the same way.

- Click in the header of Chapter 1 and click the **Link to Previous** icon in the ribbon to deselect it.

- Insert the header on the left- or right-hand side, CHAPTER I. EVOLUTION OF TWO-SURFACE FLYING MACHINE. (Copy the text from the Chapter heading.)

- On the first page of each chapter, delete the header from the previous section and copy and paste the current chapter title. Deselect **Link to Previous**.

- You can add headers to the Preface and Contents pages too.

Printing pages from a specified section

If you have divided your document into different sections and you want to print a particular page or range of pages, you must specify what section you are referring to.

For example, suppose you have four pages of "front matter" numbered i – iv in one or more different sections, followed by Chapter 1 starting on page 1.

If you specify pages 1-2 in the print dialogue box, Word will print the first two pages in the document, i.e. the title page and the page following.

If you specify pages 5-6, Word will print the two pages numbered 5 and 6, as there are no other pages in any section with these page numbers.

To print Chapter 1, pages 1-2, you must specify which section they are in.

- Double-click in the header or footer area of the first page you want to print to ascertain what section the page is in.

- Double-click in the main text to leave the header area.

- Click the **File** tab and select **Print**.

- Clear the **Pages:** box and click the little ⓘ symbol by its side, which will tell you how to specify page and section numbers.

- Type **p1s5**, **p2s5** or **p5s5-p2s5** into the **Pages:** box.

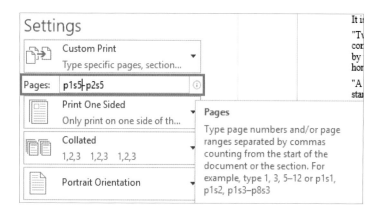

Objectives

▶ Use a template

▶ Create a fillable form

▶ Make a document read-only

Using a template

MS Word provides a collection of templates which you can use for different purposes. Shown below is a selection of templates that you can choose from when creating a new document.

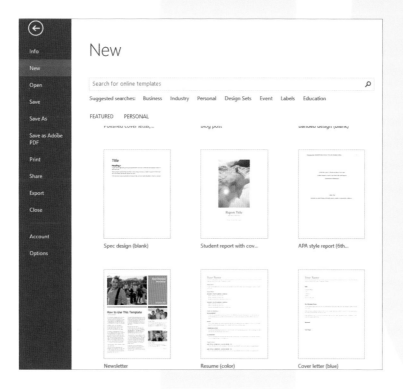

Figure 10.1:
A selection of
Word templates

A template gives you a framework which you can use to create your own document. It consists of editable text and fields which you can fill in to create a fully customised document.

This example uses the template called **Resume (color)**.

- When you click the **File** tab and select **New**, several templates are shown. You can search for other online templates by typing a search term in the box at the top of the screen.

- Load the **Resume (color)** template by clicking it, and click the **Create** button on the next screen.

- The blank template appears for you to fill in.

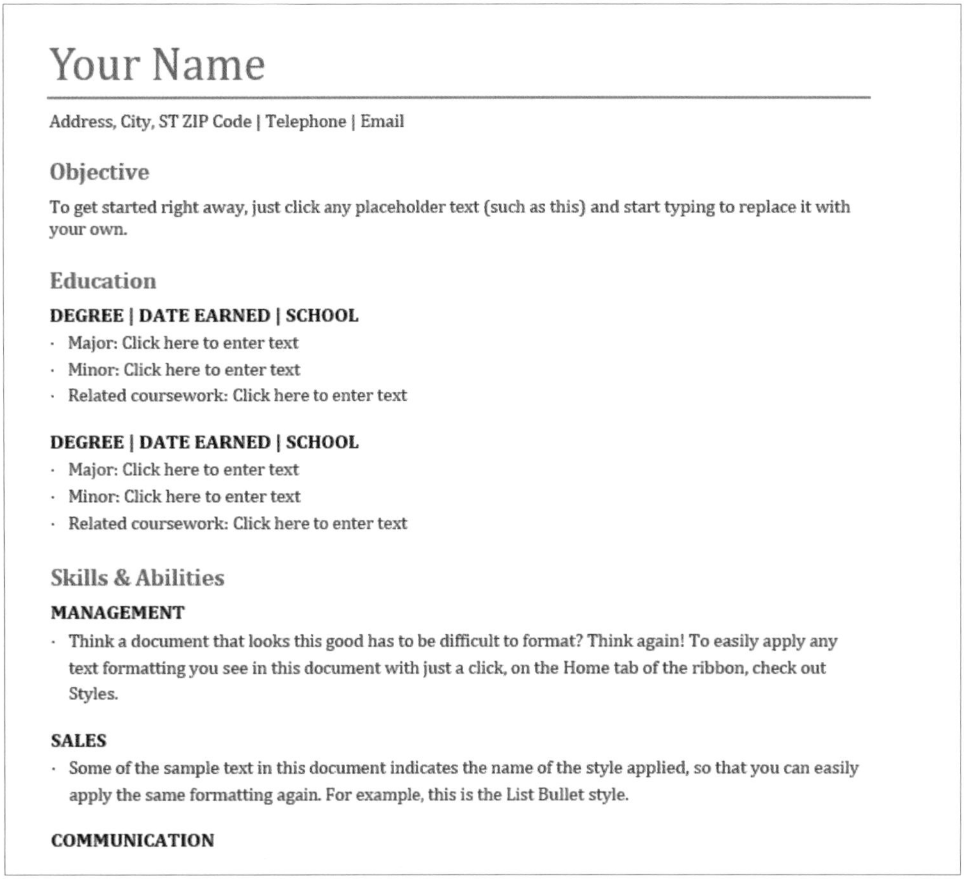

Your Name

Address, City, ST ZIP Code | Telephone | Email

Objective

To get started right away, just click any placeholder text (such as this) and start typing to replace it with your own.

Education

DEGREE | DATE EARNED | SCHOOL
- Major: Click here to enter text
- Minor: Click here to enter text
- Related coursework: Click here to enter text

DEGREE | DATE EARNED | SCHOOL
- Major: Click here to enter text
- Minor: Click here to enter text
- Related coursework: Click here to enter text

Skills & Abilities

MANAGEMENT
- Think a document that looks this good has to be difficult to format? Think again! To easily apply any text formatting you see in this document with just a click, on the Home tab of the ribbon, check out Styles.

SALES
- Some of the sample text in this document indicates the name of the style applied, so that you can easily apply the same formatting again. For example, this is the List Bullet style.

COMMUNICATION

Figure 10.2:
A blank template
suitable for a
Curriculum Vitae

Editing the blank document

Now you can edit the document, changing text, font, colour and other characteristics of the form to create your own CV.

- Save the document when you have edited the contents.

Julie Richards

45 Elm Street, Exeter, Devon. EX32 5DF | 07714 235478 | juliesrichards@gmail.com

Education

MOORLANDS SCHOOL, EXETER

GCSEs:
- Maths, English, Business Studies   A*
- Geography, Art, Computer Science   A
- Biology, Chemistry   B
- History   C

A LEVELS:
- Business Studies   A
- English, Computer Science   B

Awards

DUKE OF EDINBURGH
Gold award

LAMDA
- Acting Grade 8 Distinction

Experience

FRONT OF HOUSE STAFF | THE ORCHARD RESTAURANT TOPSHAM | AUGUST 2017
- I worked as part of a team, with frequent customer interactions. etc....

JOB TITLE | COMPANY | DATES FROM - TO
- This is the place for a brief summary of your key responsibilities and most stellar accomplishments.

Figure 10.3:
The partially
completed CV

Creating a fillable form for users to complete

An online form is a useful tool for collecting information. You can create a form for users to fill in, using either a template or a new blank document to which you can add text boxes, check boxes and other controls. The completed form can then be printed or emailed back to the sender.

The Developer tab

You will need to use the **Developer** tab ribbon for developing a form. If it is not showing in your list of tabs, you can install it as follows:

- Click the **File** tab and choose **Options**.

- In the next window, from the right-hand column, check the **Developer** tab and click **OK**.

The tab will now appear. Click it to display the ribbon:

Figure 10.4:
The Developer ribbon

A sample form using Controls

The sample form below has four questions each designed to show a different type of control. The controls used on the form are **Rich text**, **Drop-down list**, **Check box** and **Combo box** respectively.

> ## Travel Survey
>
> Please enter your name: Click here to enter text.
>
> Have you travelled abroad in the past 12 months?   Yes or No?
>
> Have you visited any of these countries in the past two years?
>
> France ☐   Italy ☐   Spain ☐   Greece ☐   Germany ☐
>
> What was the purpose of your most recent trip?   Select or enter purpose

Figure 10.5:
Sample form
using controls

Designing the form

Forms can be created for hundreds of different applications, from a multiple-choice test or a patient registration form to a customer satisfaction survey or a market research questionnaire.

The **Travel Survey** form used here has no real purpose apart from showing the function of various controls. When you create your own form for a specific purpose, you will need to think carefully about the information you are trying to collect and the responses users may give, and whether the form adequately caters for these. A finished example can be downloaded from the Exercise documents.

It is a good idea to draw a rough pencil sketch of the form first.

Creating the Travel Survey form

- Open a new document and type the heading **Travel Survey** using **Heading 1** text style.

Adding a text control

- Type the text "Please enter your name:" followed by a few spaces.

- Click the **Developer** tab and in the **Controls** group, click either the **Rich Text Content Control** or the **Plain Text Content control**. Both have an **Aa** icon. (The difference between them is that **Plain Text** can be read by any text editor, and **Rich Text** format cannot. Either will do here.)

Your form now looks like this:

Figure 10.6:
Adding a text control

> # Travel Survey
>
> **Please enter your name:**   Click here to enter text.

Adding a Drop-Down List control

- Type the next line of text, "Have you travelled abroad in the past 12 months?" followed by a few spaces.

- Click the **Drop-Down List Content Control**. (Hover the cursor over each of the controls to find out their functions.)

Figure 10.7:
Adding a drop-down
list control

> **Have you travelled abroad in the past 12 months?** Choose an item. ▾

The options **Yes** and **No** now need to be specified. If you click the arrow next to **Choose an item** in the control, you will see that the only choice is currently **Choose an item**. The options need to be changed to **Yes** and **No**.

- In the **Controls** group on the **Developer** tab ribbon, select **Properties**.

Figure 10.8:
Content Control
properties

- Select **Add** next to the list of **Drop-Down List Properties**.

Figure 10.9:
Adding an option to
the drop-down list

- Type **Yes** in the **Display Name** box. The **Value** will be filled in automatically. Click **OK**.

- Add a further item for **No**. Click **OK**, and **OK** to close the window.

- Try out your control. It still has the extra option **Choose an item**. This needs to be removed.

- Click **Properties** again from the ribbon. Select **Choose an item** and click **Remove**, and then **OK** to close the window.

Adding check box controls

- Type the following text:

Have you visited any of these countries in the past two years?

France   **Italy**   **Spain**   **Greece**   **Germany**

- Place the cursor a few spaces away from **France** and click the **Check Box Content Control** icon.

- Repeat for the other countries.

Figure 10.10:
Check box controls

Have you visited any of these countries in the past two years?

France ☐   **Italy** ☐   **Spain** ☐   **Greece** ☐   **Germany** ☐

Adding a combo box control

A combo box is similar to a list box, but with the added function that a user can type in an entry if their answer does not correspond to one of the given options.

- Type the text "What was the purpose of your most recent trip?" followed by a few spaces.

- Click where you want the combo box to appear and select the **Combo Box Content Control** from the ribbon.

- Click **Properties** and fill in the options as shown in **Figure 10.11**, deleting **Choose an item**.

Figure 10.11:
A combo box

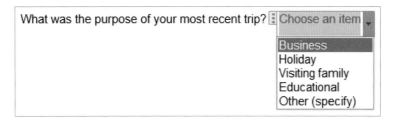

Editing a control

The text **Choose an item** shown in **Figure 10.11** can be changed, for example to **Select or enter purpose**. To do this:

- Click **Design Mode** in the **Controls** group in the **Developer** ribbon.

The fields now appear as shown in **Figure 10.12**, and you can edit any of the text.

- Select the text in the combo box and type new text **Select or enter purpose**.

- In the drop-down list, replace the default text with **Yes or No?**

- Save your form, naming it, for example, **Travel Survey**.

Figure 10.12:
Controls in
Design Mode

Adding form protection

To make the form usable, protection must be added to ensure that someone filling in the form cannot change any of the text outside the control boxes.

To add protection:

- In the **Protect** group on the **Developer** tab ribbon, click **Restrict Editing**.

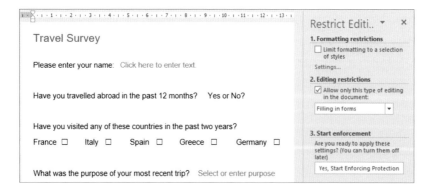

Figure 10.13:
Restrict Editing

- Under **Editing restrictions** check **Allow only this type of editing in the document**. Select **Filling in Forms** and click **Yes, Start Enforcing Protection**. Do not enter a password.

- Save your form with a different name without entering data in the controls, naming it for example, **Travel Survey (Protected)**.

- Now try editing any text on the form. It should only be possible to change the data in the control fields.

- Close without saving.

Editing the form

To edit the form, you need to first unprotect it.

- Open the blank form **Travel Survey (Protected)**.

- On the **Developer** tab, click **Restrict Editing**. The **Restrict Editing** window will appear.

- Click the **Stop Protection** button at the bottom of the window.

- Make the required changes, then click **Yes**, **Start Enforcing Protection** and save.

Making a document read-only

Sometimes you may need to make a document **Read only** to ensure that it cannot be deliberately or accidentally changed.

- Open a new document and type a sentence.

- Click the **File** tab, and the down-arrow on the **Protect Document** icon.

- Click **Restrict Editing**.

- The **Restrict Editing** window will appear. Under **Editing restrictions**, check the box **Allow only this type of editing in the document** and select **No changes**, (**Read only**).

- At the bottom of the window, click **Yes**, **Start Enforcing Protection**.

- For this example do not enter a password. If you forget the password, you will never be able to remove the **Read only** protection.

Removing Read only protection

- Click the **File** tab, and the down-arrow on the **Protect Document** icon.

Figure 10.14:
Removing read-only
protection

Protect Document

Protect Document

Certain types of changes are restricted in this document.

- Click **Restrict Editing**.

- The **Restrict Editing** window will appear; at the bottom of the window, click the **Stop Protection** button.

Congratulations – you have now progressed well beyond the basics of Word!

Appendix – Useful shortcuts and key combinations

Editing shortcut key combinations

Ctrl + **A**	Select all
Ctrl + **B**	Apply or remove bold formatting
Ctrl + **C**	Copy
Ctrl + **Shift** + **C**	Copy formatting
Ctrl + **F**	Find
Ctrl + **I**	Apply or remove italic formatting
Ctrl + **P**	Print
Ctrl + **S**	Save
Ctrl + **V**	Paste
Ctrl + **Shift** + **V**	Paste formatting
Ctrl + **X**	Cut
Ctrl + **Y**	Redo or repeat last action
Ctrl + **Z**	Undo an action
Shift + **F3**	Toggle case
Alt + **=**	Insert equation
Shift + **Enter**	Create a soft line break
Ctrl + **Enter**	Insert a page break
Ctrl + **[**	Decrease font size
Ctrl + **]**	Increase font size

Navigation shortcuts

Ctrl + **Home**	Go to beginning of document
Ctrl + **End**	Go to end of document
Shift + **F5**	Go to last place text was edited

Index